BizPlan
Express

Jill E. Kapron

JIAN Tools For Sales, Inc.
1975 W. El Camino Real
Mountain View, CA 94040
1.800.346.5426
650.254.5600
650.254.5640 Fax

http://www.jian.com

SOUTH-WESTERN
TM
THOMSON LEARNING

Australia · Canada · Mexico · Singapore · Spain · United Kingdom · United States

ISBN: 0-538-86986-0

8 9 10 MZ 03 02 01

Printed in the United States of America

Publishing Team Director: John Szilagyi
Project Leader: Susan Freeman Carson
Text Development and Production: The Oxford Associates, Inc.
Production Editor: Kelly Keeler
Cover Design: Tin Box Studio/Sandy Weinstein
Cover Photo: © 1994 J. Craig Sweat Photography
Marketing Manager: Steve Scoble

JIAN Tools for Sales, Inc.

Founded by Burke Franklin in his living room in 1986, JIAN began operations as a provider of sales and marketing brochures and direct mail vehicles. Two years later, it introduced the revolutionary BizPlan*Builder* software, winner of Success Magazine's "Editor's Choice Gold Medal Award." BizPlan*Builder*, the flagship of JIAN's line, provides business and marketing plan templates for organizing and financing a business. Now the most popular business plan software ever, BizPlan*Builder* has sold nearly twice as many copies as any competitive product, over 300,000 copies. BizPlan*Express* is the condensed version, which can get you on your way to a complete business plan even faster than BizPlan*Builder*.

What is a Jian? You might think of it this way: while a Black Belt is a master of the martial arts, a "Jian" is a master of every art—the ultimate human with extraordinary acumen, power and resourcefulness. JIAN's mission is to provide strategic building blocks to help managers build better companies—faster, easier and more economically.

All JIAN packages are developed and refined by experts with successful, real-world business experience. JIAN has gathered input from these specialists as well as commissioned accountants, consultants, lawyers and other experts for further guidance. Most of the people at JIAN, as well as the consultants and independent contractors who work for JIAN, are or have been owners of small companies. All of these materials, insights and experience have been engineered into tools and templates you can use to build your business.

JIAN continues to meet the needs of new and emerging businesses with innovative new software products including:

- Marketing*Builder*
- EmployeeManual*Maker*
- Publicity*Builder*
- Loan*Builder*
- Agreement*Builder*
- LivingTrust*Builder*
- SafetyPlan*Builder*

Welcome to BizPlan*Express*

The original BizPlan*Builder* guidelines, templates, and spreadsheets have been streamlined to create BizPlan*Express*. This *Express* business plan system is designed to help you learn to create a concise and effective plan for any business, big or small. BizPlan*Express* is half the length of the original BizPlan*Builder*. It focuses on the essential elements of a business plan and helps you create a basic plan in less time.

Investors will grill you on everything. As an entrepreneur, you may need to seek funding for your new business venture. Someday you will probably need to explain your business plan to an investor, banker, or to someone else. You must be comfortable discussing every aspect of your business and your business plan.

Managers and owners will grill you on everything. In many businesses today, team leaders and department managers are preparing business plans. Owners and managers want a clear picture of your strategies for success. You may have to define the mission, vision and strategy of your group within the larger organization. And you may have to persuade management to invest in your team and your initiatives. Whatever your needs, BizPlan*Express* gives you the tools to prepare a complete, professional business plan.

Now you have a tremendous head start. The process of developing your plan through the BizPlan*Express* worksheets and on-line templates will enable you to generate a unique plan and be comfortable discussing anything about your business. Your marketing and sales strategies will substantiate your financial projections. Your Market Analysis and Marketing Plan (see Part 2) will make the difference between a "blue sky" proposition and a viable business venture worthy of a solid investment.

Let's Get Started

Your instructor will direct you in the selection of a company you can use to develop a business plan project. BizPlan*Express* provides background information, instructions, printed worksheets, and word processing and spreadsheet templates for preparing each section of your business plan. The templates lead you through the thought process and writing process for each section of your plan. The templates have complete sentences with blanks for you to fill in for your business. Templates for non-financial sections are also provided in worksheet form so you can work in the environment of your choice to complete your plan. The financial elements of your business plan, such as your budget and cash flow statement, are illustrated in the book and included as spreadsheet files on the BizPlan*Express* disk.

When you finish a template for a section, you have all the text needed for that section. Of course, as you progress you will naturally edit, update and refine the text. If a particular passage or section doesn't make sense to you or doesn't seem appropriate for your business, then simply cross it out or delete it from the template.

Part 1, **Business Plan Basics**, is a brief reality check on writing business plans. It has years of wisdom crammed into a few pages, and it makes a lot of sense. Included in this section are the Top 20 Questions you're most likely to be asked about your business. Be sure to read Part 1 before starting in on your plan. Page 1.

Part 2, **Writing the Narrative**, has a section about each non-financial portion of the business plan:

- Title page
- Table of contents
- Executive summary
- Vision and mission
- Company overview
- Product strategy
- Market analysis
- Marketing plan

Each section has background information, instructions and a worksheet for writing that section of the plan. Page 8.

Part 3, **Completing Your Financial Plan**, has information and instructions for developing your business' financial plan. In addition to general financial advice, there are also instructions for using the spreadsheets on the BizPlan*Express* disk. Page 88.

Part 4, **Executing Your Plan**, has advice about funding and presenting your business plan. Page 112.

Appendix A, **Using BizPlan*Express***, has instructions for installing and using the BizPlan*Express* templates. Page 135.

Appendix B, **Resources**, is a list of books and articles for further research. Page 142.

There's also an index. Page 144.

Internet Access

Take a look at our web site! You'll find a variety of useful information including new products, demos, listings of professional advisors, and links to complementary products and services. You'll find us at http://www.jianusa.com.

Using BizPlan*Express* in the Classroom

The best way for you to progress through BizPlan*Express* is to select a real-world company, product, or service and complete a business plan for that firm. To make issues even more important, contact that firm and present the business plan to them at the end of the semester. This client relationship encourages the best level of critical thinking, problem solving, and concept application. Your instructor can direct you in the selection of a company you can use to develop a business plan project. Or you may decide to make up your own product or service that realistically could be launched at the end of the semester. The learning objectives, review questions, and activities throughout the book are designed to help you build your knowledge as you build your plan.

BizPlan*Express* Software

The BizPlan*Express* software package included with this book consists of word processing and spreadsheet templates that work easily with most popular Microsoft Windows programs. You can print the completed templates and use them as your actual business plan.

Throughout this text, you'll find icons like the one shown here. These icons indicate BizPlan*Express* templates.

See Appendix A, Using BizPlan*Express*, for instructions about installing and using the templates. Page 135.

BizPlan*Express* Contents

BizPlan*Express* Worksheets

BizPlan*Express* Spreadsheets

A sensible man never embarks on an enterprise
until he can see his way to the end of it.

— Aesop

Part 1: Business Plan Basics

It's hard to take a business seriously when there is little or nothing in writing about its structure, future direction, or position in the marketplace. That's why a business plan may be the most important document you'll ever write.

Simply stated, a business plan is a written document detailing the operational and financial aspects of your company. Like a road map, it helps you determine where you are, where you want to be and how you're going to get there. If it's well written, your business plan will keep you in touch with your goals, potential risks and probable rewards. Moreover, it may be the crucial factor in convincing investors or company management to give you the financing you'll need to realize your dream.

Whether you are seeking a loan, looking for an investor, soliciting management or simply using the business plan to manage your business growth, the ideas outlined in this section provide some useful tips.

Part 1 includes:

- Why Write a Business Plan?
- Components of a Business Plan
- Targeting Your Business Plan
- 10 Steps to Complete Your Business Plan
- Top 20 Questions

 **Learning Objectives**

After Completing Part 1, you should be able to:

1. Understand why you should write a business plan

2. Know the components of a business plan

3. Determine who the targets of your business plan will be

4. Know the 10 steps to complete your business plan

5. Be familiar with the top 20 most-asked questions about your new business plan

■ Why Write a Business Plan?

The first and most important benefit of a business plan is that it gives you a path to follow. A plan sets the stage to make the future what you want it to be.

A plan makes it easy to let your banker or other investors in on the action. By reading or hearing the details of your plan, he or she will have real insight into your situation if the bank is to lend you money. Likewise, potential investors can review your plan to gain a better understanding of your business and to determine if their investment is worth the risk.

A plan can be a communications tool when you need to familiarize sales personnel, suppliers and others with your operations and goals.

A plan can help you develop as a manager. It can give you practice in thinking about competitive conditions, promotional opportunities and situations that are advantageous to your business. Such practice over a period of time can increase your ability to make wise decisions.

A good business plan saves you money and time by focusing your activities, giving you more control over your finances, marketing and business objectives.

What Kind of Plan Is Best for You?

1. A **complete business plan** is necessary when you need a significant amount of funding. You'll need to explain your business concept in detail to potential backers, strategic partners or potential buyers of your company.

2. A **summary business plan** is a shorter format that contains the most important information about your business and its direction. A summary plan is great when you're in a hurry. It's usually about 10-15 pages long and is perfect for many bank loans, or simply to gauge investors' interest. A summary plan is also good for attracting key employees or for convincing friends and relatives to invest a few thousand dollars.

3. An **operational plan** is the internal document for an ongoing business. It's excellent for focusing the talents of key managers toward a common goal, and therefore should be updated at least annually. A good operating plan can do wonders for any executive's career.

■ Components of a Business Plan

The components of a successful business plan and a brief description of each section are given below.

Title Page

The title page of your business plan provides the name, address and phone number of the company and the CEO. Page 9.

Table of Contents

The Table of Contents includes a sequential listing and pagination of the sections of your business plan. Page 9.

Executive Summary

The Executive Summary is a synopsis of your business plan that summarizes the highlights of the plan. Page 10.

Vision and Mission

This is a snapshot of the present stage of your business, plus a picture of where your business is going and what it will look like, and the goals and objectives on how to get there. Page 22.

Company Overview

This section provides basic information about your company: structure, management, staffing and strategic alliances. Page 34.

Product Strategy

This section reviews your current product or service and what makes it unique and competitive. Your future research and development plans and production and distribution are part of your product strategy. Page 43.

Market Analysis

This section helps you define your market, the demographics of your target customers, competitors' products or services, and business and environmental risks. Page 53.

Marketing Plan

Your sales strategy, advertising, promotion and public relations are covered in this section. Page 68.

Financial Plan

Your company's capital requirements and the profit potential are analyzed and demonstrated here. Page 88.

BizPlan*Express* Software

Appendix A, Using BizPlan*Express*, has instructions for installing and using the BizPlan*Express* templates. Page 135.

After Your Plan Is Completed

After you have completed your plan, you will find additional useful information in this book:

- Part 4, Executing Your Plan, explains how to present and fund your business plan.

  - Supporting Documents lists a variety of additional documents you might include to substantiate your business plan, such as company brochures and resumes of key individuals. Page 113.

  - Presenting Your Plan details how to assemble, print and distribute your plan. Page 114.

  - Funding Your Plan details dozens of methods and sources for securing funding. Page 120.

- Appendix B, Resources, is a list of books and articles for further research. Page 142.

■ Targeting Your Business Plan

A business plan could be the perfect tool for you to reach the following target audience.

- Associates – to establish agreement, direction and purpose

- Bankers – to provide loans for equipment and expansion
- Business Brokers – for selling your business
- Employees – to align their efforts with yours and keep the vision of your company alive
- Investors – to supply cash for growth
- Marketing Managers – to develop detailed marketing and sales promotion plans
- Small Business Administration (SBA) – to approve low-cost business loans
- Senior Executives – to approve and allocate company resources
- Stock Offerings – to help write a prospectus for selling stock or partnership units
- Suppliers – to establish credit for inventory and materials
- Talented People – to persuade them to join you
- Yourself – to collect your thoughts, analyze your business, set goals and make decisions

Your Reader's Perspective

In addition to providing a large amount of data, your personality and spirit and those of your management team must show through—you're attracting interested people who can help you. The tone and credibility projected in your business plan will determine their response—how your reader will perceive you and your business and take action ($) on that perception. Remember this and be prepared.

Investors are often heard telling one horror story after another about a business plan "stubbing its toes" on its way into their office. One opportunity is usually all you'll get to demonstrate your competence and the feasibility of your project to your investors, senior executives or clients. These are influential and powerful people. Don't waste their time, bore them or leave them feeling dissatisfied with your work. Show them that you know what you are doing. Think in terms of return on investment. Show that you can project your company's earnings. Show that you can execute your plan.

Are Your Financial Projections Believable?

Many people think a set of financial projections is a business plan. Numbers sometimes lie, or can be used to distort the facts. Most experienced financial people know that a financial projection, no matter how honest and forthright it is, does not represent the complete picture. Conversations with bankers, investors and customers have emphasized how important it is to include several key points in your business plan: the state of your market, your product or service description in detail, market strategy, promotion and sales plans and the management team who is responsible for using the capital and driving your business toward success. All of this information provides credibility for your financial projections.

Nevertheless, the financial plan demonstrates the viability of your business, whether it's a start-up or an established company. Review your financial plan indicating your projected performance. Rethink your strategy, make changes and see the results…and be able to explain your plans.

Different financing sources look for different things and emphasize different areas—you must be prepared for all of them. Refer to Funding Your Plan in Part 4 for a list of sources. These sources make a difference to the success or failure of your business.

■ 10 Steps to Complete Your Business Plan

Depending upon your experience and time, you may choose to read the instructions and advice for each section of your business plan before filling in the worksheet or simply begin with the worksheet.

Here's a suggested procedure for using BizPlan*Express* to write your business plan:

1. For a "warm-up" exercise, begin by answering the Top 20 Questions on page 6. The answers to these questions will form the foundation of your business plan.

2. After reading Part 2, Writing the Narrative, do a fairly quick first draft on the worksheets for each section. Cross out any passages that aren't appropriate for your business. (You may want to edit the Title Page, Table of Contents and Executive Summary after completing your second draft.)

3. Follow up with research on areas for which you did not have sufficient information while doing your first draft.

4. Read Part 3, Completing Your Financial Plan, and then prepare your supporting financial statements using the spreadsheet templates. Fill in the worksheet for the financial portion of the business plan.

5. Use the templates to prepare a word-processed draft of the entire business plan. Fill in the gaps in the first draft of the plan as you go. Complete your Title Page and Table of Contents, Executive Summary and Supporting Documents. Include documents as needed. This is the second draft.

6. Have several trusted people look over your second draft for questions and their recommended changes.

7. Input any useful changes to your draft and do a final edit of your business plan. Use at least two people to independently edit/proofread your plan.

8. Input final changes. Read Presenting Your Plan in Part 4 before final printing and distribution of your plan.

9. Identify your target audience and include both a non-disclosure agreement and cover letter with your plan. (See the non-disclosure agreement worksheet in Part 4.)

10. Distribute and track your plan through phone calls or letters as needed.

■ Top 20 Questions

0-20QUES.DOC

Note: Word processing templates are shown with the .DOC extension. Depending on which installation option you select, your files may have the extension .RTF. See details in Appendix A.

Originated to help develop advertising brochures and promotional pieces, the Top 20 Questions are what most people will ask you about your business. BizPlan*Express* will help you develop and enhance your responses further in the following sections.

You can also include these answers as an initial summary for bankers or investors. You should have the answers to these questions readily available when seeking a loan or investors for your new venture.

Some of these answers may be appropriate to include in a cover letter for your business plan. (See Presenting Your Plan in Part 4.)

1. What type of business do you have?
2. What is the purpose of your business?
3. Who are your target customers?
4. What is your primary product or service?
5. What is the primary function of your product or service?
6. What are three unique benefits of your product or service?
7. What is your reason for being in this business? (What's a nice person like you doing in a business like this?)
8. What led you to develop your product or service?
9. Who is your competition?
10. How is your product or service different from that of your competition?
11. What are the top three objections to buying your product or service immediately?
12. What is the pricing of your product or service versus your competition?
13. When will your product or service be available?
14. Is this product or service used in connection with other products/ services?
15. Are you making any special offers to distributors or customers?
16. What is the key message or phrase that describes your business?
17. What are your current plans for advertising and promotion?
18. Do you have datasheets, brochures, diagrams, sketches, photographs, related press releases, or other documentation about your product?
19. How will you finance the growth of your business?
20. Do you have the management team needed to achieve your business goals?

■ Review Questions

1. What is a business plan? Why should someone in business or thinking of going into business write one?

2. Chris Jordan is starting a local catering business called PartyWorks. Who might be the key targets for the PartyWorks business plan?

3. Ozark Welding Supply is a 25-year-old company that delivers welding gas, rod, and wire to manufacturers and repair shops in a 100-mile radius. The owners have decided that they want to add a retail outlet to serve people with welding equipment at home or the very small business. What financing source would you suggest? What kind of business plan (complete, summary, or operational) should they develop?

4. How will answering the Top 20 Questions that may be asked about your business assist you in completing your business plan?

■ Activities

1. You should have a business concept in mind that you will use throughout this workbook. After you have selected a concept, work through the Top 20 Questions (0-20QUES.DOC).

2. Look at the section 10 Steps to Complete Your Business Plan (page 5). For each step, estimate hours or days to complete. Build a time line. How long do you estimate it will take to complete the ten steps?

There is one thing stronger than all the armies in the world,
and that is an idea whose time has come.

— *Victor Hugo*

Part 2: Writing the Narrative

A business plan is an action-oriented document. Many, if not most, readers will not read your plan from start to finish, at least not the first time through. You want readers to be able to quickly find the section they want and locate the information they're interested in reading within that section. Once they find what they're looking for, the information must be clear and to the point.

Part 2 focuses on writing the non-financial portions of your business plan, from the title page to the marketing plan. It covers the:

- Title Page
- Table of Contents
- Executive Summary
- Vision and Mission
- Company Overview
- Product Strategy
- Market Analysis
- Marketing Plan

Each portion of the plan is covered in Part 2. Each section has background information and instructions and a template for writing that section of the plan.

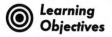 **Learning Objectives**

After completing Part 2, you should be able to:

1. Create the non-financial portions of your business plan

2. Understand the importance of having a formal title page and table of contents

3. Understand the function and components of the executive summary

4. Know how to create your own vision and mission statements

5. Understand the important role of the company overview section

6. Recognize that product strategy is a complex component involving current products, future products, research and development, and production and delivery

7. Analyze your market—define your market and profile your customers and your competition

8. Develop a comprehensive marketing plan to reach your target market

*Don't be afraid to take a big step if one is indicated;
you can't cross a chasm in two small jumps.*

— *William Lloyd George*

Title Page

The title page of your business plan should always begin with your company name, address and phone number. In addition, your title page must contain the name, address and phone number of the CEO (Chief Executive Officer).

If your plan will be distributed to several investors or bankers, you should include a copy number. This identification number will allow you to track the plans and limit the circulation to the intended audience. Keep a list of who received your business plan and when, and do appropriate follow-up by phone or mail.

Your plan should also include a confidential and proprietary statement as well as a disclaimer regarding securities.

File: 1-TITLE.DOC

You can use the BizPlan*Express* template 1-TITLE.DOC to create your title page.

Table of Contents

The Table of Contents provides a quick reference to the key sections of your business plan.

The Table of Contents should list each section of your business plan. Be sure to number the pages of your plan. It is recommended that your pagination include the section numbers followed by the page numbers, e.g., 2-1 to 2-7, instead of straight sequential numbering, e.g., 1 to 10. This will assist the reader in finding specific sections of your business plan and allow you to revise the plan more easily in the future.

File: 2-TOC.DOC

You can use the BizPlan*Express* template 2-TOC.DOC to create your table of contents.

The man who goes farthest is generally the one who is willing to do and dare.
The sure-thing boat never gets far from the shore.

— George Bernard Shaw

Executive Summary

Although your business plan begins with the Executive Summary, it is the last section you should write. In many ways, it's the most important section you will write. It provides you the opportunity to make a strong first impression on your target audience.

This section covers:

- Function of the Executive Summary
- Components of the Executive Summary
- Executive Summary Checklist
- Executive Summary Worksheet
- Sample Executive Summary

■ Function of the Executive Summary

The Executive Summary serves two important functions. First, it should convey to the reader that you have an accurate understanding of your business. It should compel the reader to continue on in order to obtain a fuller picture of your company. If it does this, then the rest of your plan will have a chance to stand on its own merit.

Second, due to time or other constraints, the Executive Summary may be the only section of your plan that some evaluators will read. If you assume your reader may have only five minutes to review your plan, what are the most important points to convey?

In either case, the Executive Summary should be brief (one to three pages) and should contain highlights of your company, its products, its markets, and its financial position and performance—both current and projected. Including knowledge of your industry, management team and financial reports, as well as your plan to pay back investors, will convince your reader that your business can and will succeed.

■ Components of the Executive Summary

The Executive Summary briefly discusses each component of your business plan: Vision and Mission Statements, Company Overview, Product/Service Strategy, Market Analysis, Marketing Plan, and Financial Plan.

Each component is discussed in depth in the rest of Part 2. It is recommended that you complete each section of your business plan before writing the Executive Summary.

■ Executive Summary Checklist

✓ Have you written all of the other components of your business plan? (If you haven't, you shouldn't begin writing the Executive Summary.)

✓ Does your Executive Summary convey to the reader that you have an accurate understanding of your business?

✓ Does your Executive Summary compel the reader to continue on in order to obtain a fuller picture of your company?

✓ Does your Executive Summary cover the most important points of your business plan?

✓ Does your Executive Summary contain highlights of your company, its products, its markets, and its financial position and performance—both current and projected?

✓ Does your Executive Summary contain knowledge of your industry, management team and financial reports and discuss your plan to pay back investors?

✓ Is your final copy of the Executive Summary one to three pages in length?

■ Review Questions

1. Why should the title page include a copy number?

2. The text recommends that the Table of Contents pagination style refer to section numbers followed by page numbers within each section. Why?

3. What is the function of the Executive Summary?

4. Carlos Martin wants to write a business plan for a mobile accounting service. He begins by writing his Executive Summary. Is this a good place to begin? Why or why not?

5. What are the components of the Executive Summary?

■ Activities

1. Set up a sample title page for your business concept.

2. The Executive Summary worksheet and template (3-EXECSM.DOC) very briefly touches on *all* of the components of the business plan. Review the form and fill out as many sections as possible. At this point do you have all the information that you need?

3-EXECSM.DOC

Vision and Mission

In 19____, [Company] ....

was [formed/created] ....

to [describe the goal of your business] ....

....

....

Overall, our company can be characterized as a ....

....

of [product and services] ....

....

Company Overview

Background

For many years people have [current use of product or service] ....

....

....

The "state of the art"/condition of the industry today is such that ....

....

....

....

We have just [product status] ....

.... of

[product/service] ....

which is used for [how product is used] ....

....

The legal form of [Company] ....

is ....
....located in

[addresses] ....

....

....

By 19......... our operation was producing [sales, units, products] ....

.... and has operated at

[status of financial condition] ....

ever since. Revenue projected for fiscal year 19......... without internal funding is

expected to be $.................... . Annual growth is projected to be .... %

per year through 19............. .

Now, [Company] ....

is at a point where [needs and goals] ....

....

....

Objectives

Revenue projected for fiscal year 19......... without external funding is expected

to be $............. . Annual growth is projected to be .... % per year through

19............ . We feel that within .... years, [Company] ....

will be in a suitable position for [company status] ....

....

Our objective, at this time, is to propel the company into a prominent market

position.

Capital Requirements

According to the opportunities and requirements for [Company] ....

described in this business plan, and based on what we feel are sound business

assumptions, our [initial/first year/total] .... capital

requirements are for $................ by [month] .... 19................ .

To accomplish this goal we have developed a comprehensive plan to intensify

and accelerate our marketing and sales activities, product development, services expansion, engineering, distribution and customer service. To implement our plans we require a [*loan/investment*] .... totaling $............ for the following purposes [*create a bulleted list of activities that are pertinent to your goals. Cross out the activities that don't apply and write additional ones as needed*]:

- Build manufacturing facilities and ramp up production and inventory to meet customer demands.
- Maximize sales with an extensive campaign to promote our products/services.
- Add retail outlets, regional marketing/sales offices, print a direct-mail catalog.
- Reinforce Customer Support services to handle the increased demands created by the influx of new orders and broader coverage of existing accounts.
- Augment company staff to support and sustain prolonged growth under the new marketing plan.
- Increase Research and Development to create additional follow-on products as well as to further fine-tune our competitive advantages.

....

....

....

....

We anticipate additional investment requirements of $............ and $............ in .... [*months/years*] .... and .... [*months/years*] to allow us to increase production capacities to meet market demand.

Management Team

Our management team consists of .... men and women whose backgrounds consist of .... years of marketing with [*list company names*] ....

.... ,

and .... years of corporate development with [*list company names*] ....

Our management team also includes .... men and women with .... years of engineering and design with [*list company names*] ....

.... ;

a chief financial officer with _____ years of [*accounting, administrative,*

merger and acquisition, banking]_____ experience with

[*list company name*]_____ .

In-House Management

_____, President

_____, Vice President of Marketing

_____, Vice President of Sales

_____, Vice President of Finance

_____, Vice President of R&D

_____, Vice President of Operations

_____, Controller

Outside Management Support

_____, Accountant/CPA

_____, Corporate Attorney

_____, [*Type of Consultant*]

Additionally, our outside management advisors provide tremendous support for management decisions and creativity.

Product/Service Strategy

Current Product

[*Company*]_____

currently offers [*list products and resources*]_____

_____ .

_____, our principal product, consists

of [*describe product*]_____

Overall our existing product line is [*give status*]_____

Our product technology consists of [describe product technology]_____

Research and Development

In response to demonstrated needs of our market, new [names of products/services]

are being developed to include [description of new features]

These new [names of products/services]

are especially useful to [describe prospective customers]

who can now easily [activity customer can accomplish]

Launches are planned for [month] 19 and [month] 19 .

In addition to our existing [products/services] , we
[have developed/plan to introduce]
follow-on products/services. [Name of product]
is a [description of product]

and is especially useful to [type of prospective customers]

who can now easily [description of how customer can use product]

Other product/services include [name of product/service]

Production and Delivery

The key factors in our [production or service]
delivery include [factors affecting production or service]

Our current [product or service]

is produced at [location of plant or by name of supplier]

Because of [describe circumstances]

our future facility will need to [expand/move/etc.] _____.

Our biggest advantage is [describe advantageous circumstances] _____

_____

Market Analysis

Market Definition

The [type of market] _____

is growing rapidly. The market for these products amounted to $_____

million in 19____ representing a _____ % growth over $_____ million

in 19____.

According to the [source of information] _____,

the overall market for the [name of your business' industry] _____

industry [worldwide/nationwide/in this region] _____

is projected to be $_____ [billion/million] _____ by the end of

19____.

The area of biggest growth in the _____ market is in

the area of _____.

Currently, the market distribution is shared by _____ participants, with

[name of top competitor] _____

considered the market leader.

In the next ____ to ____ years it is estimated that there will be more than

_____ [thousand/million] of [product] _____

distributed by [Company] _____.

The market potential for [product] _____

in these quantities—with a current retail price of [$] _____ per unit—is

approximately $_____. This translates to [Company's] _____

_____ market share of ____ % of the overall market by 19____.

Customer Profile

[Company's] _____
target market includes [types of customers] _____
_____ .

The typical customer of our products is someone who is in the _____
_____field, and who currently uses [product] _____
_____for [application/purpose] _____
_____ .

A partial list of customers includes:
_____
_____

Competition
Companies that compete in this market are [competitor 1] _____ ,
[competitor 2] _____ , and [competitor 3] _____ .
All companies charge competitive prices: [list examples and range of prices]
_____
_____ .

Key factors of [list top factors] _____
_____
_____

have resulted in the present competitive position in the industry.

Compared to competitive products (or the closest product available today), our
[product/service] _____ [can/will]_____ [describe
market's perception of your product] _____
_____ .

The ability to [describe function] _____
_____

is a capability unique to [Company's] _____
products/services.

Our strategy for [meeting/dominating] _____ the competition is
[describe strategy] _____
_____

Risk

The top business risks that [Company] ....

faces as it begins to [enter/expand in] ....

the .... market are:

....

....

An environmental risk that may cause some concern is [list top environmental risk]

....

....

Marketing Plan

Responses from customers indicate that our [name of product/service] ....

....

is enjoying an excellent reputation and we fully intend to continue this trend.
Inquiries from prospective customers suggest that there is considerable demand
for it. Relationships with [leading OEMs (Original Equipment Mfgs.), retailers, Fortune
500/1000 companies, major accounts, manufacturers and distributors] ....

....

substantiate the fitness of [Company] ....
for considerable growth and accomplishment in our industry/area.

[Company's] ....
marketing strategy is to aggressively enhance, promote and support the fact that
our products [describe product's unique features, benefits, established market position/
presence] ....

....

Sales Strategy

Because of [product's] ....

[special market characteristics] ....

_____ ,

our sales strategy includes [*description of sales strategy*] _____

_____

_____ .

Distribution Channels

[*Company's*] _____

marketing strategy incorporates plans to sell [*product*] _____

through several channels: _____

_____ .

The determining factors in choosing these channels are _____

_____ .

Our mix of distribution channels will give us the following advantages over our

competition: _____

_____ .

A partial list of [*Company's*] _____

major current [*distributors/retailers*] _____ includes:

_____

_____ .

Advertising and Promotion

Our advertising and promotion strategy is to position [*Company*] _____

as the leading [*manufacturer/service provide/distributor*] _____

in the market.

We will utilize the following media and methods to drive our message home to

our customers: _____

_____ .

For the next _____ [*months/years*] _____ , advertising and

promotion will require $_____ . On an ongoing basis we will budget

our advertising investment as _____ % of total sales.

Public Relations

During 19_____, [*Company*] _____

will focus on the following publicity strategies:

We will track, wherever possible, the incremental revenue generated from our advertising, promotion and publicity efforts. We anticipate at least $ _____ of sales will be generated directly from our promotions, and possibly an additional $_____ of indirect increase in sales through our various channels.

Financial Plan

Our objective, at this time, is to propel the company into a prominent market position. We feel that within _____ years [Company] _____ will be in a suitable position for [further expansion/an initial public offering/ profitable acquisition] _____.

Exit/Payback

The attached financial projections indicate that the exit of [name of investor] _____

will be achievable in _____ years.

The exit settlement will be in the form of [state the type of form] _____

[OR]

The increase in profits generated by [product/service] _____

will allow us to have the funds to repay the loan in _____ months/years.

Conclusion

[Company] _____ enjoys an established track record of excellent [support/service] _____ for our customers. Their expressions of satisfaction and encouragement are numerous, and we intend to continue our advances and growth in the _____ _____ marketplace with more unique and effective

[product or service] _____

A man to carry on a successful business must have imagination.
He must see things as in a vision, a dream of the whole thing.

— *Charles M. Schwab*

Vision and Mission

The essence of a business plan is to define and communicate what your company is today, where it is headed in both the short and the long term, and how the company is going to get there. Whether you are promoting and describing your existing company, a company concept or a product concept, the principles outlined in this section will apply.

This section includes:

- Looking at the Big Picture
- Present Situation
- Vision Statement
- Mission Statement
- Goals
- Vision and Mission Checklist
- Vision and Mission Worksheet

■ Looking at the Big Picture

All activities of your company should be in alignment, aimed in a certain direction. Your business may seem like this sometimes, and at other times activities may seem scattered. When writing your business plan it is crucial to know what your company is today, where it is headed in both the short and the long term, and how management is going to make sure the company gets there. This is the essence of planning.

If you are writing your business plan to outline, promote and fund a specific company concept, a product concept or a new product line, rather than for an entire existing company, the same principles outlined here will apply, although not on as global a basis. If this is your situation, you may not need to put as much time and detail into this section of your plan.

Just as important as defining your direction, you must be able to clearly communicate these concepts to many people (employees, partners, vendors, customers and potential investors) in the course of growing the business. How well this communication works affects whether the success potential of your business will be realized.

It is critical on both accounts that these words be put into writing. The work and care you invest into this section of your business plan will form a backdrop for subsequent sections. Your plan will thus have a focus and be easier for your target reader to visualize.

■ Present Situation

The starting point for any discussion of the vision of your future begins with your company's Present Situation. What is your business doing on a daily basis?

- Who is your company serving through its products and services, and how?
- What real benefits or values does your business provide today?

If you have done an honest assessment of your company's overall strengths and weaknesses, you can be more objective in your description of what your company really is, rather than what it should or might have been. Readers of your business plan want to know if you are in touch with the reality of your business situation. After all, it is the business that best works to meet the real needs of its customers over time that will survive and thrive.

After you look at the broad view of your current corporate position, similar questions should be addressed regarding specific areas. In your business plan's Present Situation discussion, briefly (a sentence or two for each area) touch on management, products, product life cycles, market environment, pricing and profitability, customers, distribution, financial resources and any other area you feel is vital. This is your best opportunity to give your target reader an accurate glimpse of your company today.

■ Vision Statement

By defining and understanding your company's future destination you help determine the feasibility of your business' success. Vision is simply a picture of where your business is headed. It describes the dream, the intended future destination of your business, based on realistic long-term projections of the present situation. It puts into brief words what the company will be like, how big it will be, what industry it will be serving, what kind of products it will be providing, and who future customers will probably be. The vision for some businesses may be described in terms of a few years into the future, while others in more mature and less volatile industries describe vision in terms of ten to twenty years or more into the future.

The vision statement can influence a wide range of people. Potential investors, employees and potential employees, partners, vendors and customers can all contribute to drive your company to success...if they buy into your vision. Your business plan needs to help facilitate this buy-in.

Putting Vision to Words

There are dangers in creating long, grand or abstract visions for a company. These visions are less believable, only vaguely understood, and most difficult to communicate and attain. The vision statement should be reality-based and should not paint a larger picture than the company has a good chance of growing into. If the vision is clearly achievable, rather than self-serving fluff, you can more readily develop a concerted team effort and build enough momentum to make it happen.

It is advisable for the owner, founder or leader of your company to take the first pass at writing a vision statement. After all, this is where the vision probably began. It should be shared with key members of senior management (and, if applicable, with the board of directors) for feedback and fine-tuning.

The vision statement should lay out a path for your company to stretch its possibilities, yet it must remain simple, believable, achievable and understood. All people involved in and associated with your company should be able to comprehend and in some way relate to the vision. Otherwise your company and its management "may wind up making more poetry than product," as a senior manager once aptly proclaimed. It is still the wisest vision of all to provide real products and services that real people will buy!

■ Mission Statement

Your company's mission statement should concisely describe, in writing, the intended strategy and business philosophy for making the vision happen. In a few sentences it conveys how all the combined efforts put into your business will move it toward its vision. It should distinguish your business from all others. Mission statements can and do vary in length, content, format and specificity.

Fred R. David, a prominent strategist, gives the following components and corresponding questions that a mission statement should answer. *

1. **Customers**. Who are and who will be your customers?

2. **Product**. What are your company's major products or services?

3. **Markets**. Where does your company compete?

4. **Technology**. What is your company's basic technology?

5. **Concern for survival, growth and profitability**. What is your company's commitment toward economic objectives?

6. **Philosophy**. What are the basic beliefs, values, aspirations and philosophical priorities of your company?

7. **Self-concept**. What are your company's major strengths and competitive/ technological advantages?

8. **Concern for public image**. What is your company's public image and standing in the community?

9. **Concern for employees**. What is your company's attitude toward its employees?

Depending on the size and complexity of your business, you may feel that only a few of the above components need to be directly addressed in order to produce an effective mission statement for your company.

Some companies communicate their mission in only a sentence or two. As an example, the one-sentence version of JIAN's Mission Statement is as follows:

> JIAN's mission is to be the preferred source for results-oriented, project-specific business development tools to empower entrepreneurs and business managers to streamline common and complex management tasks for the success of their companies and the benefit of the world.

---

* Source: David, Fred R. Strategic Management. Ohio: Merrill Publishing Company, 1989.

Other companies use a couple of paragraphs or more to detail their mission statement. Whatever the length or format of their statement(s), every word should count. A mission statement should be both highly descriptive and inspirational. It should be broad enough to cover a range of strategies and objectives, while calling attention to the top priorities.

A mission statement, even more than a vision statement, should be a team effort. It should accurately reflect the operational direction and spirit of your business. If the mission statement is not supported by the various managers and departments within the organization, then it may well be inaccurately or incompletely reflecting the true direction of your business. For a reality check, your mission statement should be revisited regularly, at least before the annual planning or budgeting process.

Need for Written Statements

Many business people dismiss the need for written vision and mission statements, considering the process as mere linguistic exercises with little or no impact on the real workings of the business. However, many studies and informed sources indicate that companies (and individuals) with written vision and mission statements have a far higher success rate than companies that do not. Conversely, the vast majority of companies that fail have not had written vision and mission statements.

■ Goals

Goals translate thought into action. They focus people and activities. Achievement is meaningful if the reason for achieving matches what is important. The Wall Street Journal showed a survey of the top goals for Americans in the '90s. The breakdown was as follows:

- Spend time with family and friends: 77%
- Improve themselves intellectually, emotionally or physically: 74%
- Save money: 61%
- Have free time to spend any way they please: 66%
- Make money: 61%
- Travel or pursue other hobbies or personal experiences: 59%

Business-wise, goals must align with the big picture of your company. This section of your business plan provides information on the business goals that will be achieved as your company operates according to its mission statement on the way toward reaching the stated vision of its future.

Business Goals

While the mission statement conveys how your company will conduct its business, the goals state which accomplishments will need to take place to move the company in the direction of its vision.

Goals must measure a predetermined level of performance to be achieved within a specific time period. Each major business goal should be tied into the long-range plans of the business. It should be written in a manner that supports the company's mission statement. As an example, suppose that your mission stated that your company was to become the manufacturer of the highest quality widget on the market. An aligned goal might be worded as follows:

In order to become the manufacturer of the highest quality widget on the market, defective products returned by customers will be less than 1% for the year.

Each specific objective should be written so that the goal that it is supporting is expressed. Goals should focus on getting results by making the organization work more effectively. Goals serve as a contract between people and build responsibility, accountability and growth. Consistently setting and attaining appropriate goals is an indicator of a business person's ability to define and run his or her business. Well thought-out and supported goals in a business plan indicate to the audience that the business is on the right track.

Good goals:

- Deal with vital issues
- Contribute to profit or productivity
- Are measurable and specific
- Tie into company vision/mission
- Are stated as end results
- Offer challenge but are realistic
- Are controllable by you
- Are time limited
- Are rational
- Provide a return on investment
- Have financial objectives
- Position the business for growth

For the majority of businesses, there are many basic goals an owner might choose to adopt. The following is only a sample of what an entrepreneur has to choose from.

- Market Penetration
- Market Maintenance
- Market Expansion
- Diversification
- Utilization of Capacity
- Specific Net Profit Percentage
- Profit Maximization
- Asset Productivity and Return on Equity

Methods for Building Goals

A good way to begin setting goals for your business is with sales and marketing goals. The first stage is goal-based on the bare minimum dollar value of sales your business must reach to break even based on expenses you have researched and expect to incur. Once you have completed those calculations based on expenses, you can compare your "must reach" break-even sales level with demographic studies to determine if the target market has enough demand. The Market Analysis section later in Part 2 discusses demographics further.

Using this same strategy, you can set your next goal to earn a specific return on the dollars you invested in starting your business. An example would be if you used $10,000 of your own money to start the business and you want to earn a 20% return on that investment. This means you would have to break even plus earn a $2,000 profit. Again, you can compare this projected sales volume to the demographics to determine if the market has sufficient demand.

You can take this approach and use varying expense amounts based on different locations, different capital requirements based on those different locations, and varying returns on investment. By doing projections this way, you are able to compare various locations and return on investment requirements that you have established as goals. Instead of trying to set an arbitrary sales figure, you can set concrete goals and then determine if the market can support those goals.

In preparing these projections by month and for future years, you should also consider any seasonal fluctuations in sales, the effect of inflation on your expenses and sales prices, and any debt repayment you might have on borrowed money. For further discussion on projections, see Part 3, Completing Your Financial Plan.

If you have an existing business, these projections are a little easier to prepare. You can base your expense projections on actual expenses your company has incurred, rather than on researched estimates, and you can base your sales goals on past sales growth performance. You can use the same techniques as a new business if you want to set specific return-on-capital requirements for your existing business. Instead of comparing these goals with demographics, you can compare them with past performance to see if they are realistic.

Summary

If a company's vision, mission, and goals are aligned, the company is well on its way to success. If your company is far from this level, do not despair. Well over 99% of companies are in this same situation. The key here is to use the company vision to motivate—thus ensuring your company's long-term success.

■ Vision and Mission Checklist

✓ What is your company's present business situation regarding products and services, benefits or values?

✓ What is your dream for your company?

✓ How large will your company be?

✓ What industry will your company be serving?

✓ What kind of products will you be providing?

✓ Who are your current and future customers?

✓ Is your vision statement reality based?

✓ Does your vision statement accurately describe the growth that your company can achieve?

✓ Has a key member of senior management provided feedback and fine-tuning to the vision statement?

✓ Does your mission statement describe the intended strategy and business philosophy for making the vision happen?

✓ Does your mission statement distinguish your business from all other similar businesses?

✓ Did a team of managers from various departments write the mission statement?

✓ Are you regularly revisiting your mission statement to determine if you are meeting the concepts included in it?

✓ Do the goals of your company clearly state the accomplishments that need to take place to move the company in the direction of its vision?

✓ Is each major business goal tied into the long-range plan of the business?

✓ Are the goals focused enough for getting results by individual organizations?

✓ Do you have a sales goal?

✓ Do you have a marketing goal?

✓ Are your goals appropriate, acceptable, feasible, flexible, measurable, specific and understandable?

■ Review Questions

1. Why does this portion of the business plan involve a review of the current situation?

2. How can a vision statement help reveal the feasibility of a business' success?

3. Who should write the vision statement? Why?

4. Why should the vision and mission statements be written documents?

5. What is a mission statement? How is it different from a vision statement?

6. How do business goals relate to the mission statement?

■ Activities

1. Using your own business concept, write a real or hypothesized present situation using the form in this section.

2. Using your own business concept, create vision and mission statements using the form provided in this section. Use the vision and mission checklist starting on page 27 to guide the development of these statements.

4-VISION.DOC

Present Situation [*]

Company

[Company] ....

was founded in 19 .... and is presently in its [start-up/R&D/growth] ....
.... stage.

[Company] .... can best be described as

currently being in the business of [business description] ....
....
....

In recent times our key strengths have been [describe business strengths]
....
....
....

Management

Most of our management team is in place, however, we require a [Manager Title]
....

to complete our team by [month] .... 19 .... Also, we are currently

hiring .... employees to fill the following job titles: [list job titles] ....
....
....

Products and Services

At present our [product]...

is in the ....

stage. Our current product line/service is in need of [describe product need]
....
....
....

---

*   Briefly take stock of your present situation regarding the company, management, products and services, market environment, pricing and profitability, customers, distribution, financial status. One or two pages should be sufficient.

   Describe the current condition of the business—a present-day "snapshot." If you're in the concept stage, tell what you are doing now to build the foundation of the business.

   Clearly describe the one current dominant driving force of your business. Examples are: product/service offered, satisfying a market need, manufacturing, profit and income, technology, and client/customer base.

Market Environment

The marketplace is [undergoing rapid changes/has been stagnant] ....

.... for .... years. We are now poised to

[describe market push] ....

....

....

Pricing and Profitability

Current prices are [holding/eroding/increasing] ....

and profits are [holding/eroding/increasing] ....

Customers

Current customers are using [product] ....

for [describe product uses] ....

....

They are requesting that we [make improvements/introduce a new model/etc.]

....

Distribution

We have .... service centers, retailers, manufacturer's representatives, sales

people working out of .... offices, territories in .... states, countries.

Financial Status

Current cash available is $ ....

Our Current Ratio is: Assets/Liabilities = ...

Our Quick Ratio is: [Cash and Equivalents + Accounts Receivable + Notes Receivable

divided by Total Current Liabilities =] ....

Vision and Mission [*]

Vision Statement

By 19 .... [Company] ....

will be a highly visible company known as the best [product] ....

---

*   *Ask yourself – Where do you want to go with the business? What do you want to be? What direction(s) will the company be taking? What do you want (personally and financially) five to ten years from now?*

   Clearly describe the following future dominant driving forces: product/service offered, satisfying market need, manufacturing, profit and income, technology and client/customer base.

   Be creative while keeping your description believable, understandable, motivating and achievable.

in the [category/name] ....

industry. We will have developed [product name/line] ....

and marketed these products in the [marketing channels] ....

.... ,

becoming [a/the] .... leader in [product category] ....

Sales will exceed $.................. and [Company] ....

will actively be promoting [product name] ....

....

Mission Statement

In order to achieve our Vision, [Company] ....

commits to the following:

[Company's] ....

Mission is to provide innovative, practical and top-quality products that save time

and improve the way people do [describe action] ....

We believe our first responsibility is to the [customer category] ....

who uses our products and services. Our strong financial position will enable us

to [describe goals] ....

....

In carrying out our day-to-day business we strive to:

1. Treat our employees with [describe characteristics] ....

....

2. Follow the philosophy that our customers are [describe how company treats

customers] ....

....

3. Be considered as [describe company position within community] ....

....

Through a long-term commitment to this mission, we will be known as a

company that [describe how you hope market will perceive company] ....

....

Our customers, vendors and employees see [Company] ....

as offering [describe offerings] ....

....

....

Goals

In order for [Company] ....

to attain its vision in the manner described in our mission statement, the

following primary strategic goals need to be achieved:

Corporate: By [month] .... 19............., [Company] ....

will [describe corporate goal(s)] ....

....

....

Products: By [month] .... 19............. , [Company] ....

will develop [describe product-related goal(s)] ....

....

....

We expect to replace [competitive/existing products or services] ....

.... by .... % by 19........... .

Market: By [month] .... 19............., [Company] ....

will reach [describe customer-related goal(s)] ....

....

....

We will have an active customer base of over .... customers. To reach

these customers we plan to add .... [retailers, distributors, service centers]

.... per [month/year] .... and we will have a total of ....

[retailers, distributors] .... by 19............. . We will expand our

marketing efforts to the regions of ....

....

and generate additional revenue as high as .... % more than current

levels.

Sales: By [month] .... 19............., [Company] ....

will [describe sales-related goal(s)] ....

....

....

Our products will be prominently displayed in over .... retail stores and influential establishments, with salespeople and consultants being knowledgeable and supportive of our products and company.

For 19_____ total sales will exceed $ _____.

For 19_____ total sales will exceed $ _____.

For 19_____ total sales will exceed $ _____.

For 19_____ total sales will exceed $ _____.

Operations: By [month] _____ 19_____, [Company] _____ will produce [describe operations/production-related goal(s)] _____ _____.

Compared to past performance of [product/service name, type] _____ _____ in the [industry name] _____ industry we intend to _____ _____ _____.

Finance: By [month] _____ 19_____, [Company] _____ will [describe finance-related goal(s)] _____ _____ _____.

We will carefully evaluate and plan investments and budget expenses to generate a consistent _____ % pretax profit. Based on a _____ % market share for our [product name] _____ by 19_____, we estimate our return on investment to be _____ %.

Many years ago Anaheim, California, was mostly a giant orange grove,
but Walt Disney saw Frontierland, Tomorrowland, Fantasyland…
imagine what it took to explain Disneyland.

— Anonymous

Company Overview

The company overview sets the stage for your business plan. This section describes the legal structure of your business as well as your management team.

This section includes:

- Legal Business Description
- Management Team
- Board of Directors
- Staffing
- Strategic Alliances
- Company Overview Checklist
- Company Overview Worksheet

■ Legal Business Description

Company Name

A business is a legal entity and requires a company name that is approved and registered with your local government prior to the opening of a new business. The legal name of your company may be different than the name used in dealing with customers. If you intend to operate under a name other than your own, you must file a Fictitious Business Name statement in order to be "doing business as" (For example: John Smith, d.b.a. Sun & Fun Bike Touring). The fictitious business name is usually more descriptive of the product or service. Used with a company logo, the fictitious business name may also promote recognition for your product or service.

The Legal Forms of Business

The three basic forms a business can take are proprietorship, partnership, and corporation. Each form has distinct advantages and disadvantages concerning ease of start-up, tax considerations and legal liability. In recent years a new hybrid status called a Limited Liability Company (LLC) has become popular in some start-up situations. The LLC is discussed later in this section.

Proprietorship

The easiest way to open your business is as a sole proprietorship. This form has a single owner and the only legal requirement to establish it is a local business license. Just as easily, you can dissolve or close the business at any time, and it automatically ceases upon your death. As the sole owner, you have absolute authority to make all the decisions.

The major disadvantage of a proprietorship is that you are personally liable for all debts and contracts. There is no distinction between personal and business debts, so if the business cannot pay its bills, creditors can sue to collect from your personal assets. Income from the business flows directly through to you and is taxed at the individual rate. You do not pay yourself a salary; your income is the profits from the business. There is also no carry back or carry forward of losses. Although last year you did not have to pay any taxes because of a loss, this year you will have to pay the full taxes on your profits; you cannot cancel out this year's profits with last year's losses and pay taxes only on the net total for the two years.

Partnership

The second form is the partnership, of which there are two types: general and limited. In a general partnership, two or more people combine money, property, skills, labor or any combination of resources to form the assets of the business. Each partner is a co-owner and is entitled to a share of profits and losses. The percentage of each owner's share is described in the partnership agreement, which is not required, but should exist in writing. It should describe the percent ownership of each partner, the management responsibilities of each, how the profits or losses of each will be distributed, how the owners can withdraw capital or money from the business, how partners can be added to or allowed out of the business and what happens if one of the owners dies. As in proprietorship, there are no legal requirements to open other than local licenses to operate and the Fictitious Name if you operate under a name other than the collection of partners' names. Unless otherwise specified in the partnership agreement, the partnership dissolves immediately upon the death, insanity or insolvency of any one partner. Again, the disadvantage of the partnership is that every partner is fully responsible for all debts and contracts. Any business obligation entered into by any one partner is binding on all partners, regardless of the amount they invested.

The second type of partnership is a limited partnership, which consists of at least one general partner and one or more limited partners. In a limited partnership, only the general partners have any decision-making authority or any type of input as to the operation of the business. The limited partner contributes capital only and cannot participate in the running of the business. Unlike the general partners who are fully liable for all debts and contracts of the business, the limited partners cannot be personally sued because of the debts of the business. The most that limited partners can lose is their investment, but the general partners can lose their investment and be sued for personal assets. The limited partnership is organized under state laws and certain documents must be filed with the state.

In both forms of partnerships, all income is passed directly through to the individual owners in percentages described in the partnership agreement. The same tax rules as a proprietorship apply with regard to profits being taxed at the individual rate and the taxing of capital gains. However, in a partnership, losses are carried back three years and forward for fifteen. The partnership files a complete return with the IRS which includes a Form 1065 (a business profit and loss statement). Each individual partner will file a Schedule K-1 and a Schedule E for his or her percentage of the profits.

Corporation

There are two kinds of corporations: a C-Corporation and an S-Corporation. In both, ownership of the company is evidenced by shares of stock, which are readily assignable or transferable (you can use them for collateral on a loan or sell them at any time). In theory, corporations are separate legal entities from the owners. They can open checking accounts, borrow money, and operate just as a person might in the business world. Because of this unique structure, the business continues forever despite changes in ownership or management. Also, corporations offer what is called "limited liability" to the owners, which means the owners cannot be sued for the debts of the business unless they have personally guaranteed those debts. Therefore, the potential loss for you, the owner, is limited to the capital that you invested. (Capital does not have to be money. It can be property, machinery, skill, or labor.) Debtors can sue the corporation only and can claim only the assets of the business. For this reason, banks will usually require most closely held corporate owners to co-sign or guarantee any loans.

Ultimate control or management of the company is in the hands of the shareholders, who generally meet once a year and who elect a Board of Directors. The Directors usually meet to oversee major corporate policies. They appoint Officers who hire management to run daily operations. In a small company, the shareholders are also the Board of Directors and management.

In a proprietorship or partnership, the company has only two ways to get new capital: personal money or money borrowed from a bank. A corporation, however, can sell shares of stock, borrow directly from the public by selling corporate bonds or borrow from a bank.

Because a corporation is considered to be an individual identity, it must file an IRS tax return and pay taxes on its profits. Unlike a proprietorship or partnership, profits do not flow directly through to the owners. If the owners are also company employees, their salaries appear as expenses on the company's books and are reported as wages on the individuals' 1040 form. If the company earns a profit after all expenses (including owners' salaries) and the owners want to take that money out of the company, then those profits are paid to the owners as "dividends" and are reported on the individuals' 1040 tax return along with Schedule B (interest and dividend income).

This is one disadvantage of a corporation. Not only are the profits taxed on a corporate basis, but if they are distributed to the owners, they are taxed again at the individual level, creating "double taxation." A corporation shares the same tax advantage as a partnership in that it can carry losses back three years and forward fifteen years. These losses are used to offset profits and limit the company's tax payments. If the business had losses last year and did not pay any taxes, you could carry those losses forward to this year's tax return and offset any taxable profits.

An S-Corporation differs from a C-Corporation in regard to a few tax considerations. In order to be an S-Corporation:

- Your company must be domestic.
- There can be only two classes of stock: voting and nonvoting.

- Only individuals may own stock.
- There cannot be any nonresident aliens as shareholders.
- The company cannot own any subsidiaries or be part of any affiliated group of companies.
- There can only be a maximum of 35 shareholders.

An S-Corporation has the same legal liability properties as a C-Corporation and the shareholders must vote or elect to become an S-Corporation. They then must file a Form 2553 with the IRS.

An S-Corporation files a full corporate tax return as C-Corporations do (Form 1120), only they use a Form 1120S. However, the return is for informational purposes only. *The profits or losses flow directly through to each shareholder based on the number of shares owned.*

The shareholder reports profits as supplemental income on a Schedule E. Therefore, not only does the owner report wages on the 1040, but he or she also reports the distribution of profits as supplemental income. The advantage is that the S-Corporation does not pay taxes on the profits and double taxation is avoided. All profits must be passed through to the owners and taxes paid on those profits, even if the owners do not actually take the money out of the business. The final tax advantage is that, unlike the proprietorship and like the C-Corporation, an S-Corporation can carry losses forward or backward to offset previous or future profits. Given these tax considerations, when most people incorporate they do so as an S-Corporation as long as they expect to operate at a net loss. In this way, losses are passed through to the individual owners. However, once the company starts to become profitable and to retain those profits, the S-Corporation election is dropped to prevent taxes on that money retained in the business.

Limited Liability Company (LLC)

During the '90s, many states have begun adopting a designation for businesses called a Limited Liability Company. LLCs are a hybrid of the above types, providing tax benefits equivalent to those of a Limited Partnership and protection equivalent to that of a C-Corporation or an S-Corporation. LLCs can be privately held companies only, although they can be changed to C-Corporation status if you want to go public at a later date.

As of the end of 1994, 48 jurisdictions, including the District of Columbia, have LLC legislation in place. Only Massachusetts, Hawaii, and Vermont are without such a law. Contact the Association of Limited Liability Companies in Washington, D.C., for more information.

■ Management Team

The management team provides the leadership for your business and must include combined strength in both management and technical areas. The management team should be selected in such a manner that talents are complementary rather than overlapping or duplicated. You must ensure that all the key areas necessary to accomplish the goals and objectives of the company are within the strengths and talents of your management team.

Early on in your business, you will want people who are capable of handling multiple functions. As your company grows, your requirements will call for more specialization within the management team. A combination of experience, technical skills and energy will serve your company well. Recommended reading on this topic: *The Greatest Management Principle in the World*, by Michael LeBoeuf, Ph.D.

■ Board of Directors

The Board of Directors is usually vested financially in the company and in a large company may take the form of venture capitalists. They may also bring specific business experience to the management team.

■ Staffing

Understanding the strengths and weaknesses of your staffing is important to the investor. Although you may not have all your staff in place when you begin, a plan of action that addresses how and when you will fill the gaps is required. A new business may turn to consultants and other professionals for specific areas of expertise. Both small and large companies should seek the professional services of an attorney and an accountant during business start-up.

■ Strategic Alliances

Strategic alliances can strengthen and broaden your potential market as well as add talent to your management team. Some of the alliances you may seek include Original Equipment Manufacturers (OEMs), joint marketing, third-party supplier, or joint developer. For more information, refer to Part 4, Funding Your Plan.

■ Company Overview Checklist

- ✓ Has your local government agency approved and registered the name of your company?
- ✓ If your company's name is different from your own, have you filed a Fictitious Business Name statement?
- ✓ Have you reviewed the different forms of business and determined which is appropriate for your company?
- ✓ Have you established a management team that provides leadership for your business in both management and technical areas?
- ✓ Do the strengths and talents of your management team match the goals and objectives of your company?

✓ Does your Board of Directors bring specific business experience to the management team?

✓ If your staffing is not complete, do you have an established action plan to share with your prospective investors?

✓ Have you considered strategic alliances to help strengthen and broaden your potential market or to add talent to your management team?

■ Review Questions

1. If your business is a sole proprietorship, how is it taxed by the Federal government? What are the implications if you have a loss?

2. What is the difference between a general and a limited partnership?

3. Tom Herman is trying to decide whether his new metal plating company should be a C-Corporation or an S-Corporation. The shareholders are Tom and his three sons. He expects the company to have sales of about $500,000 per year with slow annual growth (5%) but to show annual losses of about $75,000 for the first three years due to start-up costs. What do you suggest?

4. What is a Limited Liability Company? Why would a firm organize as an LLC?

5. Included in the company overview is a description of your management team. Why? What should you emphasize in this description?

■ Activities

1. Fill out the legal business description section of the Company Overview worksheet (next page) or template (5-COMPANY.DOC), making a decision about the legal form of your proposed business. Are you able to complete the Government Regulations section? How could you find out the details that you need to complete this section?

2. Using the section of the worksheet or template that discusses the management team, what are the key positions for your company? What type of credentials should these people have?

3. Using the section of the worksheet or template that discusses staffing, what additional staff will be needed in your first year? What outside support personnel will you need?

5-COMPANY.DOC

Legal Business Description

Company Name

The legal name of [Company] ....

is [list full name of company as listed on your registration with your local government]

....

....

Legal Form of Business

The legal form of [Company] ....

is [Sole Proprietorship/General or Limited Partnership/C-Corporation/S-Corporation/Limited

Liability Company] ....

....

....

....

Business Location

The business location of [Company] ....

is ....

....

....

Management Team

Our management team consists of .... men and .... women. Their

backgrounds consist of .... years of marketing with .... years of corporate

development with [former employers' names] ....

....

.... ,

[number] .... people with .... years of engineering and design with [former

employers' names] ....

....

.... ,

and a chief financial officer with .... years of accounting, administrative,

merger and acquisition and banking experience with [former employer's name]

....

Officers and Key Employees	**Age**	**Stock**
...., President	....	....
...., Vice President of Marketing	....	....
...., Vice President of Sales	....	....
...., Vice President of Finance	....	....
...., Vice President of R&D	....	....
...., Vice President of Operations	....	....
...., Controller	....	....
...., Corporate Attorney	....	

Of the _____ people who make up the corporate staff, there are _____ founders who hold the following positions:

[Name] ...., [Title] ....

[Name] ...., [Title] ....

[Name] ...., [Title] ....

Each founder has been provided with _____ % of the original stock issue.

(Resumes of officers and key employees should be provided in the Supporting Documents.)

Board of Directors

An outside Board of Directors, including highly qualified business and industry [professionals/experts] ...., will assist our management team in making appropriate decisions and taking the most effective action; however, they will not be responsible for management decisions. Their names and background highlights include [name, background] ....

....

....

....

Staffing

[Company's] ....

development team recognizes that additional staff is required to properly support marketing, sales, research and support functions.

Currently, [Company] ....
is composed of .... people; .... will be required to meet the
demands of the projected market over the next five years: ....

....

....

....

*(for example, management [number] , marketing [number] , sales [number] , engineering
[number] , customer relations [number] , administration [number], manufacturing [number] ,
assembly [number], repair [number] , field service technicians [number], maintenance
[number]).*

Strategic Alliances

[Company] ....
has formed some very important relationships with major companies in the
[industry name] ....
industry. The following is a list of existing relationships such as OEM
relationships, joint marketing agreements, third-party supplier agreements, and
joint development efforts:

....

....

....

....

....

Some men see things as they are and ask, "Why?"
I dream things that never were and ask, "Why not?"

— *George Bernard Shaw*

Product Strategy

This section describes the company's products or services in detail. Determining your future products, projected development, and how you will produce and deliver to your customers are key aspects of Product Strategy. This provides the real bloodline for your company.

This section includes:

- Current Product
- Research and Development
- Production and Delivery
- Product Strategy Checklist
- Product Strategy Worksheet

■ Current Product

The current product description in your business plan should highlight the unique, distinct or improved features and benefits of your product. Many companies begin with a unique idea for a product or service that grows in scope over time. These product insights, and subsequent methods of exploiting them, often provide a compelling story. This section is of special interest to bankers or investors. They will want to know what sets your product or service apart from the competition, how well you produce your product, and what new trails your company may be blazing.

Proprietary Technology

Proprietary technology is a new or unique product, application or base of knowledge (sometimes called intellectual property) in the market that may be protected under patents, copyrights, trademarks, etc. Your company gains this legal protection when registering with the U.S. Department of Commerce's Patent or Trademark Offices. The registration of your product provides you with legal protection and recourse in a court of law if a competitor tries to copy your idea.

A large portion of a company's worth is often in patents, copyrights and trademarks. If your company deals in these areas, it is important to keep your legal status current and to maintain a thorough inventory of your intellectual property.

Useful Features/Benefits

Customer satisfaction is increased if the customer understands the features and benefits of your product. Features and benefits must address the customer's needs and wants and must distinguish your product from the competition.

The product should be designed with the customer's needs in mind. How well and how cost-effectively these features actually produce desired benefits and results to your customers will determine whether your product (and company) experiences boom or bust.

■ Research and Development

All companies need ongoing product and service development. Your target market, competitors and current technologies are always changing. To maintain a competitive edge, you must keep on top of new developments that will affect your business. Some of the questions to consider are:

- Do you have a plan for a new product or new technology?
- Have you established milestones to track your development?
- Have you listed your accomplishments (example: prototype, development, lab testing, etc.)?
- Have you determined all the true costs of your product development efforts and are these costs for research, testing and development, and so forth in line with your budget?
- What are your competitors spending on R&D?

Both small and large companies need to allocate resources to R&D. This may range from staffing a complete department to research customer needs and develop new products to simply keeping abreast of industry changes through publications and conferences.

Product Selection Criteria

As your company grows, selecting your new products or services becomes a bigger gamble. When you had an idea, you put it together and then tested it to see if it sold. With the marketplace becoming more demanding, competition becoming fiercer, and development and marketing costs soaring, present and future product cycle times generally require more thorough evaluation before selecting new items to develop.

More ideas and concepts are being created now than ever before. If your company has put together its vision, mission, goals and objectives (as discussed in the Vision and Mission section) you will have a big head start on the product selection process. With these planning tools in place, certain concepts will fit more readily than others, and your company focus will be easier to maintain.

Writing a Product Selection Criteria for your company may prove to be one of your wisest investments of time and effort for your management group. First of all it can pay off in wisely selected, profit-rich products or services for development. It can also save your company both financial losses and considerable grief by facilitating the wise discarding of losing product concepts that may burden your company.

The factors that should be covered in your selection criteria include financial benefit to company, relatively low investment requirements, positive ROI, fit with present strategy, feasibility to develop and produce, relatively low risk and the time required to see intended results.

Your finished Product Selection Criteria may be very short and to the point. Or it may cover a wide range of product questions as they relate to the various departments in your company. By including a Product Selection Criteria in your business plan, you show the world that you recognize what your company can produce and that you understand that product focus and execution will carry your company to the profit levels that are envisioned.

Planned Products

After you have presented your current products and how your company decides on its new products, it's time to give a preview of your upcoming hits. Your product intentions and projections should be described in the same detail as your current product or service offerings. After all, the target reader of your business plan is usually more interested in what you foresee than what you have done. This is where the target reader can assist your company's efforts in some way—ideas, investment, management assistance or materials.

Not only do you want to lay out your product plans in this section, but you also want to show how you will achieve them. Investors are exposed to dozens or hundreds of ideas each year. Most often they are unimpressed until they see a good idea with an excellent plan of execution. In your business plan, show the reader both your planned product concepts and how the products will be completed and delivered.

■ Production and Delivery

This section discusses any proposed site location, costs of your product, facilities and logistics. The emphasis must be on the productive use of capital, labor, material resources, manufacturing processes, vendor relations, experience and distribution requirements. Statements are needed that indicate initial volume and expansion requirements, as well as product/process complexity, uniqueness and costs.

Production

At this stage you need to explain how you are going to make your future product or deliver your future services. Determining your equipment, material and labor requirements, as well as their price and availability, can be critical factors in the production process. Other considerations include alternate sources/materials, inventory requirements, and care and handling of hazardous materials.

You need to determine the full capacity of your present facility and how your new product plans will translate into manufacturing schedules. How will new product plans affect the way production is done now? Let the reader of your business plan know that you've done your homework and that your production capabilities will not be overrun by the proposed products selected for future development and production.

Costs

To determine the cost of your product, it is important to quantify your business costs in terms of production rates, capacity constraints, or required quality assurance and safety programs. Include quantity discounts, if applicable.

In evaluating the cost of the same product from other companies, you should determine why and how your costs are more competitive. This information will be important to the banker or investor who is looking at the return on investment. If subcontract or assembly work is required, list parts, vendors, lead time, costs, etc. Include information on how the future product cost will rise.

Facilities

The manufacturing facility provides needed space for initial production and expansion to meet projected demand. Site selection includes the following considerations:

- Room and cost for expansion
- Land and construction costs
- Transportation cost and route access for common carrier
- Risks and insurance
- Packaging and material costs and availability
- Labor pool availability, skills, costs
- Local ordinances, licensing and permit requirements
- Government assistance (roads, training, exemptions, etc.)
- Government restrictions and requirements (OSHA, NLRB, etc.)
- Community attitudes toward business and manufacturing
- Continued operating costs (utilities, communications, etc.)

Packaging and Transportation

The primary function of a product package is the protection and safety of the product. The package must be designed to protect the product during transportation over a specific period of time in varying climates. Finally, a package can be an effective marketing tool by differentiating your product from that of your competition. Both the packaging and the transportation of your product convey an image to the customer and must be balanced with the cost, availability and competitive products on the market.

Product Fulfillment

Product fulfillment is an important part of customer satisfaction. Providing a channel to monitor and manage the delivery, billing, warranty and repair of your products will ensure customer satisfaction and repeat sales. Some or all of these services can be supplied directly by your company. Increasing numbers of businesses are contracting some of these services to companies specializing in these areas.

■ Product Strategy Checklist

✓ Is your product registered with the U.S. Department of Commerce's Patent or Trademark Offices?

✓ Do the features and benefits of your product address your customer's needs and wants?

✓ Does your business plan describe how your company will react to competition, change in market, etc.?

✓ Does your company have resources allocated to Research and Development?

✓ Are you referring to your company's stated vision, mission, goals and objectives when selecting new products?

✓ Are you researching how your product can be regularly improved in order to maintain its competitive position, market value and price point?

✓ Can you communicate both your planned concepts and how the products will be completed and delivered in your business plan?

✓ Do you know how your product will be produced and delivered?

✓ Do you know the cost of your product?

✓ Have you considered all of the site selection factors when considering the location of your product's production facility?

✓ What type of packaging does your product need?

✓ How can your customers reach you if they have comments or problems with your product?

✓ How will your product be shipped?

■ Review Questions

1. What is "proprietary technology?" Why register it?

2. The Pet Accessory Manufacturing Company supplies pet toys, treats and grooming products to a wide variety of wholesalers and retailers across the country. They are setting up a formal Product Selection Criteria to analyze new product ideas. What selection criteria would you suggest as guidelines?

3. The Pet Accessory Manufacturing Company is projecting rapid growth and planning a new manufacturing facility. What should be some key site selection criteria for the new facility?

4. What is product fulfillment? Why might you choose an outside provider for this service?

■ Activities

1. Use the Current Product section of the Product Strategy worksheet or template (6-PRODCT.DOC) to describe your product, its features and history.

2. Using the Product Strategy Return on Investment and Useful Features/ Benefits section of the worksheet or template, look at the product from your customers' point of view. After you have filled out this section, determine the single most important advantage or benefit that your product brings to your customers.

3. Does your company have a plan for its research and development strategy? Fill out the Research and Development section of the Product Strategy worksheet or template. Why would a form such as this impress potential investors?

6-PRODCT.DOC

Current Product

[Company] .... currently offers the following products: ....

....

....

[Product name] .... , our principal product, consists of ....

....

Development of [new products, existing product upgrades, spin-off products] .... is in progress and future products are planned.

The first product developed by [Company] .... is called .... and was introduced in 19 ....

Since then, we introduced .... in 19 .... , and then [brief history of your product line up to today] ....

....

....

Proprietary Technology

Our products are protected under the following:

....

....

....

Return on Investment

For most customers, [product] .... will pay for itself in terms of ....

....

within .... months, because of ....

....

Regarding cost savings, [product] .... will save our customers money in terms of ....

....

Useful Features/Benefits

The major benefits of the combination of all [Company's] ....
products are improved ....
through .... and
....

Research and Development

Much of the time and effort at [Company] ....
during the past .... [year/period] .... has been spent on research
and [product/process] .... development. During 19 ....
[Company] ....
spent approximately .... % of sales revenues on R&D. Our plans for 19 ....
and beyond call for an [increase/decrease] ....
in R&D spending to .... % of sales.

[Company] ....
is regularly examining roles that new products will play in the growth of the
company. In order to promote the speed and effectiveness of our future new
product development efforts, [Company] ....
management is committed to the following: [list your commitments]

....

....

....

These commitments will span a period of .... [months/years] ....
and cost in the range of $ ....

Product Selection Criteria

Because marketing is [our single largest/a large] ....
expense and it is where [most/much] .... of our effort is applied,
focus on our customer is a very important criterion. The idea is to keep our
customers forever by continually offering them a valuable product or service,
thereby diminishing our costs of reaching and appealing to them. Wise product
selection is therefore critical to [Company's] .... success.

We at [Company] .... realize that
the cost of development projects is getting increasingly expensive. To assure the
best possible product decisions we have implemented the following criteria for
evaluating and selecting projects: ....

[Company] _____ provides products to assist customers with [customer need] _____

_____ .

Our _____ products help reduce time, effort and expense by _____ %, and easily retail for $ _____ to $ _____ each.

[Company] _____ can implement product or service using [off-the-shelf parts] _____

_____ .

Planned Products

[Company] _____ plans to continually develop new products and enhance existing products. In response to demonstrated needs of our market, new products or services being developed in the near future include

_____ , _____ and _____ .

Additional [concepts/plans] _____ for follow-on [next generation] products include [product name] _____ .

[New product 1] _____
development [will begin/has begun] _____
on _____ 19_____ , and will require the following resources [staffing, materials, tooling, capital equipment, technology, new processes] _____

_____ .

The targeted release of [new product 1] _____
is for _____ 19_____ .

[New product 2] _____
development [will begin/has begun] _____
on _____ 19_____ , and will require the following resources [staffing, materials, tooling, capital equipment, technology, new processes] _____

_____ .

The targeted release of [new product 2] _____
is for _____ 19_____ .

Exhibits

For additional details, the following product-related documents are included in Supporting Documents: _____

_____ .

Production and Delivery

Production

Key factors in the [manufacturing/service delivery] ....
process are ....
....
....

[Raw/prefabricated] .... materials, components,
and subassemblies required for production are ....
....
....

Costs

We take advantage of economies of scale by [describe advantageous situations]
....
....
....

In comparison to other companies, [Company's] ....
products are [reproduced/completed] .... quickly
and economically by [describe how process/techniques accomplish this] ....
....

Comparative analysis shows these figures to be [higher than/lower than/in line with]
.... competitors.

This is due to the fact that [describe circumstances] ....
....
....

Our overall costs will remain [higher, lower, or in line with competitors] ....
....

Facilities

The manufacturing facility [*is/will be*] _____ located in _____

_____ .

This location [*provides/will provide*] _____ needed space for

[*initial/current*] _____ production and expansion to meet

projected demand over the next [*periods*] _____ . Our current

production capacity, including internal and external production, is _____

units per [*week/month/year*] _____ .

Due to anticipated increases in demand up to _____ units per [*week/month/*

year] _____ , additional facilities will be needed by [*month*] _____

19____ . Selection of the future site includes the following considerations:

_____

_____ .

Product Fulfillment

Product fulfillment is an important part of customer satisfaction. [*Company*]

_____ utilizes [*our x group/an external resource*

named x] _____

to monitor and manage the delivery, billing, repair, warranty and repair of our

products to ensure customer satisfaction and repeat sales.

To improve on operating efficiencies, we plan to use _____

fulfillment company. Their facility is "state of the art" and their customer record

is excellent. We can avoid hiring more employees, expanding our telephone and

computer systems, as well as save on shipping costs.

During the past _____ [*months/years*] _____ this [*group/vendor*]

_____ has demonstrated outstanding abilities to

_____ .

Their capacity is expected to be sufficient to handle our fulfillment needs for the

next _____ years.

Transportation will be [*truck/train/air cargo*] _____ .

Comparative costs show that [*describe differences and results between your shipping*

procedures and your competitors'] _____

_____

_____ .

He who excels at resolving difficulties does so before they arise.
He who excels in conquering his enemies triumphs
before threats materialize.

— Sun Tzu, The Art of War

Market Analysis

The need to discuss consumer behavior or individual habits is not always clearly evident. However, you must remember that no matter what type of business you are in, the final decision to buy or not buy is made by an individual. The better you understand the decision-making process, the better you can sway that decision. This section describes the existing marketplace in which you will introduce your company and products.

This section includes:

- Market Definition
- Customer Profile
- Competition
- Risk
- Market Analysis Checklist
- Market Analysis Worksheet

■ Market Definition

This section describes what is known about your target market. Several key components of this analysis include an industry analysis, a market segment analysis, an analysis of your competitors' strengths and weaknesses and discovery of unexploited opportunities.

Industry Analysis

An industry analysis begins with collecting information on the size, growth and structure of the industry, as well as target market coverage, marketing objectives, marketing mix and tactics. This information can be used to monitor changes and exploit weaknesses in the marketplace that can give your company a competitive edge.

Market Segment

Within the industry, the market segment defines the market even further by product feature, lifestyle of target consumers, season, etc. Sources such as industry analyses, census reports and trade journal studies help you define your market. To become the market leader in your product or service, your company must capture the biggest portion of sales in its market segment.

Strengths and Weaknesses

In identifying the strengths and weaknesses of your competitor's product, you are evaluating the competitor's coverage of the market and its success in meeting customer demand. By exploiting this weakness, you can improve both your product and your position in the market and convey that you are (or will be) strong where your competitors are weak.

Unexploited Opportunities

Based on your marketing analysis, you may discover additional niches and opportunities to explore. Often a successful product can be leveraged through new distribution channels, licensing, packaging, etc. Identifying your top market opportunities will help you focus your marketing efforts.

■ Customer Profile

Knowing exactly who you're selling to is crucial to obtaining favorable response from your investors. The customer profile may include consumer adoption, economic factors, demographics, psychographics and influencers.

Consumer Adoption Process

The consumer adoption process is based on the idea that certain kinds of people will accept and use your product in different stages. These classes of adoption in the order of greatest willingness to try your product are: innovators, early adopters, early majority, late majority, and laggards. Each group generally has different traits that separate it from the others, such as age, race, family stage, income or geographic location. The groups also tend to read or listen to specific media and prefer different types of sales information.

Economic Factors

Economic factors are those that affect how people spend their money. The more money an individual has in savings, the more income available for leisure items such as travel, entertainment and sporting goods, and the greater potential to purchase higher-priced durable products such as cars, appliances and housing. Issues for consumers include level of personal debt, income expectations, taxes, interest rates, and savings.

Demographics

Demographics are based on research by the national census, local governmental agencies and private firms. These studies list such items as average income, average age, average family size and a variety of other information about consumers who live in a given geographic area. Excellent sources for demographic studies include your local Chamber of Commerce, the local newspaper, your state's Department of Commerce and the local library.

As a business owner, you must develop a "profile" of your primary customer or customers. These will be the people you believe have demand for your product or service and will be making the purchase decision. For example, in the scuba diving industry, one of the major publications is *Skin Diver Magazine*. The media kit for the magazine states that the "average" subscriber fits the following profile:

Male	86.0%
Female	14.0%
Average Age	34.7 Years
Attended College	82.7%
Average Household Income	$48,000

Professional/Managerial	68.4%
Traveled Overseas In Last Three Years	60.6%
Average Amount Spent On Diving In Past 12 Months	$1,598
Average Investment In Equipment	$1,710

Although this "average" subscriber is not characteristic of all scuba divers, you now have a customer profile on which to base your product line selection (depth and breadth), pricing objectives, promotional message, media channels and location selection.

Influencers

Another consideration in profiling your customer is to understand who influences purchase decisions. There are people who will:

- **Initiate** the inquiry for your product,

- **Influence** the decision(s) to buy,

- **Decide** which product or service to buy, and

- **Permit** the purchase to be made (sometimes the decision-maker and the permitter are the same person, but the decision-maker [who is often the Chief Financial Officer (CFO)], will sign the paperwork after other managers have submitted their recommendations).

Your presentation and proposal must appeal to all of the above people.

■ Competition

Two hikers were in the woods when suddenly a bear appeared.
One quickly took off his pack, pulled out his sneakers and put them on.
"You don't think you can outrun that bear do you?" asked his companion.
"No," he replied, "I just need to outrun you!"

It is important that you are aware of the many competitors perceived by your customers (consciously or otherwise). Competition not only comes from companies in the same industry, but also from other sources interested in your customers' money. For example: a swimming pool contractor not only competes with other swimming pool contractors, he competes with a customer's interest in a vacation, a new car, a new roof, a tennis court, etc. If you acknowledge these competitors and develop marketing strategies to propel your product not only ahead of others in your industry, but to the top of your customer's priority list, you will impress investors and take a commanding lead in your business. As you proceed through this section of BizPlan*Builder*, you will find many ways to improve your marketing strategy.

Evaluating Competition

It is important to know as much about your competitors' businesses as you do your own business. Here are some areas you should know about your competitors' product in comparison to your own.

Products

How do your competitors' products compare against your own, using the same criteria you used when evaluating your own product: color, size, price, etc.?

Organization

What are your competitors' organizations like? Can they make fast and accurate decisions? Will they respond quickly to changes you make? Are their management and staff competent? Are they leaders or followers in the market? How are they funded? Do you consider them to be viable competitors in the future?

Track Record

Customers will often choose a contractor or supplier because of its track record. How does your record compare to that of your competitors? Are they well known in the industry? An assessment of your stability compared to that of your competitors can be a real selling point to your customer, especially if you're selling a product that will require future servicing.

■ Risk

> *Every noble acquisition is attended with its risk;*
> *he who fears to encounter the one must not expect to obtain the other.*
>
> — *Metastasio*

Any discussion of the business environment must include the various kinds of risks. In researching risk, it is important to remember that it is impossible to anticipate all possible risks and alleviate them. The best you can do is to identify as many of them as possible and anticipate solutions to handle them before they occur. The best strategy to alleviate risk is to diversify. Use multiple suppliers, sell multiple products, attempt to keep up with new technologies and purchase insurance for those risks you can insure against, such as fire, theft and illness.

Risk can be broken down into two major categories: business and environmental.

Business Risk

Each industry has its own set of unique business risks. For example, some industries have high capital needs, others have a seasonal business cycle, and still others depend on a limited group of customers and suppliers.

Cost Structure

The first and perhaps the largest risk is the cost structure of the industry. This is directly related to the amount of fixed assets or capital required to operate your business. As discussed earlier, the amount of capital required is determined by the type of business you own and the structure of the market. In general, the more capital your industry or business requires, the larger your fixed expenses will be. If you wanted to compete with General Motors, you would need tens of millions of dollars to open your business. You would need to purchase or build a large factory and buy an expensive amount of equipment to produce automobiles. You would have debt and rent payments that would be fixed whether you produced 100,000 cars or you produced five cars. The dollars you would lose each month when not producing and selling your break-even volume of cars could rapidly force you out of business.

Competition and Industry Growth

Competition from the national brands or from present or new regionally based companies poses a risk to your company. If the market for your product continues to grow, the major national companies will likely devote greater resources to this segment. Developing a niche in the market, competitive pricing and customer service will minimize this risk.

Product Liability

Product liability insurance is a necessary evil in today's business environment. A large damage award against a company not adequately covered by insurance could adversely affect its financial position.

Profit Margin

Profit margin (the percentage of net profits to sales) versus the volume of sales is another type of risk. A good example of this risk would be to compare a grocery store to a jewelry store.

The grocery store sells its entire inventory every other day; however, net profit margin is only 1%. The business makes its money through high sales volume. The grocery store owner can determine changes in customer demand quickly and adjust for those changes within a few days. The jeweler, on the other hand, holds a piece of jewelry on average 90 days before she sells it. Because of the amount of profit she makes on each individual item, she only has to sell a few large items to equal the profit of the grocery store. However, risk lies in the jeweler's inability to detect changes in demand quickly and to adjust her marketing strategies for these changes quickly. The grocery owner can see a slowing in business within two days and adjust for it immediately. The jeweler will need 90 days to make those same adjustments. The only way to minimize the profit-volume risk for the jeweler is to have surplus cash to support operations until she can adjust her buying habits.

Seasonal Business

Is your business a seasonal one or are your sales steady throughout the year? If your business is highly seasonal, you risk having to estimate your inventory and cash needs as the season begins, matures and closes. Typically, in the retail clothing business, you need to order your fall inventory in June, your winter inventory in September and so on. Your risk is twofold. You face the possibility of buying too much inventory and not being able to sell it or of buying too little inventory and selling out early. The second part of the risk is that customer attitudes change, and the styles you ordered may not be popular.

Complementary Industries

You also need to understand how your business depends on complementary industries. If you were a plumbing contractor or a hardware store owner, your business would prosper or starve depending on how the housing industry performs. When new homes are in demand, the housing industry grows and your business has the opportunity to succeed. However, as interest rates go up, tax laws change and new home demand declines, you face declining sales over which you have no control. The best way to lessen your dependence on any one industry is to expand (diversify) your business.

Substitution

Vulnerability to substitution is a risk that your business might face. You need to see your industry in the broadest possible way. By doing so, you should be able to foresee changes. Instead of being hurt, you can take advantage of them to further expand your business.

Suppliers

If you depend on any one or just a few suppliers, they can control your business. If they raise their prices, you can be trapped into paying those increased prices. In a low inflationary economy, you might not be able to pass those price increases on to your customers. If your supplier decreases his trade terms from 60 days to 30 days, your cash flow will be hurt without your having any control. Finally, if your supplier has only a limited inventory, his ability to meet your demands might be restricted. The best way to minimize supplier risk is to spread your purchases over a number of suppliers. The more you depend on a single supplier, the more risk your business faces.

Customers

Some of the same risks associated with a limited number of suppliers can apply to your customers as well. A good example is the lawn mower manufacturer whose only customer is a major retail chain. As the manufacturer faces rising costs of production, he attempts to pass those costs along to his customer. However, because the retail chain knows that it is responsible for 100% of the manufacturer's sales, the chain can refuse to pay the increased prices. The manufacturer is faced with no sales or sales at the old price and greatly reduced profits. The best strategy is to have as many credit-worthy customers as possible. Although it is advantageous to have guaranteed sales and know you will be paid for them, it is not a favorable trade-off to lose control of your pricing to your customer.

Personnel and Management

Success of the company is dependent upon its ability to attract and retain qualified personnel. Certainly in the initial stage, success also depends on the continued service of the founder and President, as well as other key executives. While continued employment of these individuals cannot be guaranteed, various incentives (including contracts) can be used to encourage their continued participation and minimize the risk of their departure.

Environmental Risk

Your business will also face risks that are not limited to the industry you operate in. An economical downturn or revised tax laws are examples of environmental risks that can affect a wide range of companies.

Economic

Adverse changes in prevailing economic conditions can have a negative impact on the company's projected business. In a recession, consumers decrease their expenditures and retailers are less inclined to make capital investments.

Economic risks such as inflation, recession and rising interest rates affect the bottom line. You cannot alter these risks, but you can decrease the effects they will have on your company by understanding the impact of each. Perhaps the best strategy is diversification, offering numerous products or services to multiple market segments.

Weather

The weather can be a substantial risk to your business. You need to assess how changes in climate such as temperature and rainfall will affect your business. Included in this category is the potential for catastrophes such as fire, floods or drought. The best ways to avert these risks are good planning, good management and proper business insurance coverage.

Legal and Government

Almost without warning, a local ordinance can invalidate your business license, restrict your business operations by zoning laws or condemn your property in the public interest.

As with the legal risk, the business may be dependent on government regulations or contracts that affect your product. Staying abreast of legal issues facing your industry through industry publications will warn you of any significant changes.

■ Market Analysis Checklist

✓ Have you conducted an industry analysis?

✓ Have you conducted an analysis of the market within your company's industry?

✓ Have you identified the strengths and weaknesses of your competitor's product?

✓ Have you determined how you can turn your competitor's weaknesses into your company's strengths?

✓ Have you developed a customer profile?

✓ Have you analyzed your competitor's business and product?

✓ Have you researched the business risks to your company?

- The cost structure of your industry
- Competition and industry growth
- Product liability
- Profit margin
- Dependence on complementary industries
- Vulnerability to substitution
- Limited number of suppliers
- Limited customer base
- Personnel and management issues

✓ Have you researched the environmental risks?

- Economic conditions
- Weather
- Legal and governmental regulations

■ Review Questions

1. Why would a prospective lender want an industry analysis in your business plan?

2. Your firm has developed a revolutionary new coffee brewer. It is superior in delivering great coffee taste, brewing speed, and heat retention for the brewed pot. Which category of consumer in the adoption process will your firm pursue? What promotion method will you use?

3. What is demographics? Why is this information important?

4. Taking a broad view of competition, who or what would be the competition for a new twelve-screen movie theater being built in your neighborhood?

5. Assume you are a toy manufacturer, supplying several lines of games, preschool toys, dolls and action figures to Toys 'R Us, Wal-Mart and Kmart. What specific business risks might you face?

6. Assume you operate a long-haul trucking company. What environmental risks might your company face?

■ Activities

1. Fill out the Industry Analysis section of the Market Analysis worksheet (next page) or template (7-MKTANL.DOC) for your company. The information can be found in the library in business census information (Federal or state) or through industry trade associations.

2. Who is your customer for your product or service? Using the Customer Profile section of the worksheet or template, describe your typical customer.

3. Assume your new company is marketing a state-of-the-art car alarm. Use the Demographics section to describe your customers.

4. Looking squarely at potential business risks, fill out the Risk section of the worksheet or template for your company.

7-MKTANL.DOC

Market Definition

Industry Analysis

The _____ market is growing at a rapid rate. The market for these products amounted to $ _____ million in 19_____ — representing a _____ % growth over $ _____ million in 19_____ .

Referenced sources agree that the major trend is for _____ _____ _____ .

The trend has been toward the development of [*products*] _____ _____ .

The overall _____ market for the _____ industry is projected to be $ _____ [*million/billion*] _____ by the end of 19_____ . The overall market potential for [*product category*] _____ is estimated to be $ _____ million by 19_____ , and the [*additional products*] _____ portion of this market is estimated to be $ _____ million.

The area of greatest growth in the _____ market is in the area of _____ .

Market Segment

Key points in defining the market segment for [*product*] _____ are _____ ,
_____
and _____ .

The major market segments are:
[*Segment 1*] _____
and [*Segment 2*] _____ .

These products have been successfully distributed in many areas of the industry. Competitive products in this market are [*produced/provided*] _____ by [*competitor 1*] _____ ,
[*competitor 2*] _____ ,

and [competitor 3] _____ .

In the next _____ to _____ years it is estimated that there will be more than
_____ [thousand/million] _____ of [products] _____
distributed by [Company] _____ . The market
potential for [product] _____
in these quantities—with a current retail price of $_____ per unit—is
approximately $_____ million. This translates to a market share of _____ % of
the overall market.

Of the _____ customers, approximately _____ % will [buy/use/want/expect]
_____ [product] _____ to help
them to [deliver their work/maintain x/expedite their production/reduce costs/etc.] _____
_____ .

_____ of these [products] _____ will have a
_____ capability, and about _____
of those [products] _____ will require [other
features] _____ .

Strengths

In terms of product strength, [product] _____
has several distinct advantages over the competition: _____
_____
_____
_____ .

In marketing, our most powerful assets are _____
_____
_____
_____ .

Weaknesses

There [is/are] _____ handicaps inherent in our product. The
only notable marketplace disadvantages are _____
_____

and those are because [explanation and how to overcome] _____
_____
_____ .

Other known threats include [*environmental, corporate weaknesses, etc.*] _____

_____

_____ .

Opportunities

The upside potential for _____ and

[*our products*] _____ in

[*each of the currently addressed markets*] _____

_____

over the next two years is _____

_____ .

Unexploited Opportunities

An altogether new application for this product would be tapping _____

_____ markets.

Further opportunity for our product exists in _____

_____ market(s).

Still another possibility for development involves _____

_____

_____ .

Customer Profile

The most typical customer for our product is someone who is in the _____

_____ field, and who currently uses [*product*]

_____ for [*application/purpose*] _____

_____ .

It is likely that potential customers are going to be familiar with [*similar products/*

products that your new one will replace/your type of product] _____

_____

and that they will readily accept our new _____ ,

provided that we [*approach/educate/contact*] _____ .

Complementary products already in use by our customers are [*other products that*

work with yours] _____

and are seen as a tremendous help in [*compelling customers to acquire our product/use*

our product] ....
....

Demographics

On a separate page in your business plan, list different types of customers, title, power, viewpoint, position, emotional and practical influences and education. It may be appropriate to include several types of customers in your demographics, for example, Homemaker, Senior Executive, Young Married Couple, Wealthy Rural Family, Older Couple or Elderly. The first sample list is appropriate for a business customer and the second for an end-user customer.

Title: ....

Power: ....

Viewpoint: ....

Position: ....

Emotional Influences: ....

Practical Influences: ....

Education: ....

Limitations: ....

[Target Customer] ....

Age: ....

Income: ....

Sex: ....

Family: ....

Geographic: ....

Occupation: ....

Attitude: ....

Competition

Companies that compete in this market are [competitor 1] .... ,
[competitor 2] .... and [competitor 3] ....
All companies mentioned charge competitive prices [list examples and range of
prices] ....
....

The major strengths and weaknesses of our competitors are [price/location/
quality, etc.] ....
....

The major competitors' objectives and strategies are _____
_____
_____ .

The major competitors' most likely response to current [economic/social/culture/
demographics/geographics/political/governmental/technological/competitive trends]
_____

affecting our industry will be [list response of competitors] _____
_____
_____ .

Our products or services are positioned relative to our major competitors by
[price/delivery/location/etc.] _____
_____
_____ .

New firms entering and old firms leaving this industry affect our product [list how
this affects your product] _____
_____
_____ .

The nature of supplier and distributor relationship in this industry is [the supplier
and distributor effect on your product] _____
_____
_____ .

Competitive threats today come from [other companies or industries/new or entrenched
technologies/foreign countries/etc.] _____
_____

and _____ .

In all comparisons, [Company's] _____ products
provide more features and have superior performance than do competitive
products. In most cases, the number of differences is substantial. A complete
technical comparison is available.

[Competitor's] _____ [competitive] _____
product does not provide the same capabilities in a situation

where [describe circumstances] ....
....
....

Competitive Roundup

Create a chart that illustrates how your company's product compares to the competition in several key areas. Key areas to analyze for each company could include sales, share of market, estimated advertising budget, product line, quality, technology, advertising effectiveness, sales force excellence, distribution, manufacturing efficiency, industry standing, future potential, seriousness of competition, number of employees, greatest strength, and key weakness. For each product, issues include price, size, capacity, ease of use, installation, range, appearance, quality, design, useful life, trade-in value, technology, support, responsiveness, efficiency, warranty, on-time capability, and upgrades. Rank each area from one to five.

Risk

Business Risk

[Some or all of these risks may not be applicable to your situation.]

[Company] .... will need a [certain level of investment]
...................................to [open facility, expand production, and so on] ....
....

This new [facility/division/expansion] ....
will increase our capacity and increase our potential capacity by a factor of
.... In conjunction with this expansion, [Company]
.... significantly increased our marketing expense
and overhead. Margins of profit will be [lower] .... % [for a forecast number of
months or years] ....

The sale and consumption of [product] ....
has increased dramatically over the past .... years and [Company]
.... and other [product makers/providers]
.... are increasing their capacity in order to meet
this growth. There can be no assurance, however, that the growth will continue
at the present rate, or at all, and the demand for [product] ....
may not keep up with increases in supply, in which case [Company]
.... may face heightened competition and be
unable to sell sufficient quantities of our product to maintain our volume and
profit margin.

Product Liability

[Company] _____ has _____ liability insurance and will continue such coverage if available at a reasonable cost. However, future increases in insurance premiums could make it prohibitive for us to maintain adequate insurance coverage. A large damage award against [Company] _____ , not adequately covered by insurance, would adversely affect our financial position.

Environmental Risk

Economic

The economic risks affecting [Company] _____ are

_____

_____ .

The best strategy for [Company] _____ is [*diversification, offering numerous products or services to multiple market segments*] _____

_____

_____ .

Weather

[Company] _____ has provided [*planning/ good management/x insurance coverage*] _____ to protect against catastrophic weather such as fire, floods or drought. Despite these precautions, a major natural disaster could affect our business by causing

_____ .

Legal and Government

The State and Local ordinances or zoning laws that may impact our product are

_____

_____ .

[Company] _____ will stay abreast of legal issues facing [*industry*] _____ through [*industry publications*] _____

and _____

_____ .

Man's mind stretched to a new idea never goes back to its original dimensions.

— Oliver Wendell Holmes

Marketing Plan

This section discusses the overall market strategy. The marketing plan is your strategy to sell your plan to the customer as well as to the potential investor or banker.

This section covers:

- Marketing Strategy
- Sales Strategy
- Distribution Channels
- Advertising and Promotion
- Public Relations
- Marketing Plan Checklist
- Marketing Plan Worksheet

■ Marketing Strategy

Strategy can be defined as the science of planning and directing large-scale operations, specifically of maneuvering forces into the most advantageous position prior to taking action.

It is important that this section of your business plan follow the definition of strategy because it will help you specifically define your marketing and sales activities, strengths and direction. This portion of your business plan will enable you to appropriately respond to business conditions and opportunities.

A sound business plan requires a full understanding of the various types of industries, the competitive nature of the industry, and the various risks a business can encounter.

You need to determine the specific industry you are competing in. Although this might not seem important, it can be a decision that affects your company for years to come. By defining your industry, you are also defining your competition.

With this information, you can lay out your marketing plan to let your targeted market know what service or product you offer and how they can obtain it.

■ Sales Strategy

Positioning

All decisions are made by individuals, and all individuals are motivated by emotions. In the business environment, those emotions might be self-improvement, greed or the desire to impress others. Many of the same branding techniques used to convince consumers hold true for business customers as well. Positioning means how your customers perceive your company or product relative to your competitors.

Pricing

As might be expected, price is one of the most effective marketing tools you use to promote your business. Price conveys image, affects demand and can help target your market segment.

When considering what price to charge for your product or service, realize that price should not be based on production plus some profit. Rather, price should be based only on the value of your product or service to the customer! If that price does not generate the necessary profits, then changes must be made or the product line discontinued.

- How do we set prices? Is there a policy?
- Is the pricing competitive?
- Is there perceived value (it costs more, therefore it must be better) inherent in higher prices?
- Are prices based on costs—standard markup?
- Why are prices higher or lower than those of competitors?
- How elastic (the effect of pricing on demand for product) is the market for these products? How does consumer positioning affect elasticity?
- See also the Break-Even Analysis discussion in Part 3, Completing Your Financial Plan (page 100).

Pricing should follow directly from the company's overall goals and objectives as established by the owners. Every marketing strategy will have its own related pricing strategy.

A wealthy and respected man once said that he looked around at what his competitors were charging and charged a little more. Don't be too quick to discount or go for the low-price leader position. Low-price leaders are incredibly efficient, massive marketers (i.e., Wal-Mart). Many marketers like to emphasize the "offer" as the leading factor in sales response. Any salesperson can give away a product, and a competitor will surely displace your lowest price. Put yourself in your customer's position... relative to your price, isn't getting the job done far more important?

Pricing Strategies

One strategy is to "skim the cream" in the introduction phase by charging high prices when competition and substitution are minimal. Another strategy is to "match competition" by pricing slightly under competition to expand market share. A final strategy is to substantially underprice the market to exclude competitors. These strategies can be categorized into three areas: profit margin, sales and status quo goals.

Profit-Oriented Goals

Profit-oriented goals include a specific net profit percentage or profit maximization. The first is a percentage goal and the second is a dollar value goal. The first goal might be to obtain a 10% net profit on sales and would bring in $10,000 on sales of $100,000. The second would attempt to earn $15,000, a higher profit, on sales of $200,000, which would be a 7.5% (lower) return.

Sales-Oriented Goals

Sales-oriented goals attempt to reach a specific dollar or unit sales growth objective, regardless of profit percentage or value. A sales-oriented goal might also be to obtain a specific market share. Typically, these goals are used to introduce a new product or a new market. Profit goals can be established later when the company has a consistent sales volume and customer base.

Status Quo Pricing

Status quo pricing is an effort to match the competition and not "rock the boat." This is usually the goal in a mature market where competition can be based on other competitive marketing features such as promotion, place and packaging.

Discounts

When choosing a pricing strategy, in addition to the basic price of the product, you can offer discounts on single-order quantities, cumulative quantity orders or on specific products. The owner might choose to use seasonal discounts to move more product during slow times of the year. Discounts can be used for either consumer goods or industrial products. Perhaps the best known discounts are the "frequent flier" discounts being offered by the airlines.

Trade-in Allowances

Trade-in allowances are an effective way of lowering the final price to the customer without actually lowering the list price. Trade-in allowances are given for used goods when similar new products are purchased. They are standard in the automobile industry and in other industries that deal in industrial and durable goods.

Coupons

Coupons are another effective way of tailoring your pricing strategy for the consumer market. Coupons can be mailed directly to consumers' homes, delivered in local papers or offered at the point of purchase. Many cost-conscious consumers shop only for those goods where they can use discount coupons. Coupons are an effective tool to reach various markets with the same product through pricing.

Sales Terms and Credit

Included in pricing strategy are sales terms and credit. Sales terms allow customers to take a discount if the invoice is paid within a specified time period. A typical discount might be 2/10, net 30. This means the customer can take a two percent discount if the invoice is paid within 10 days, but the entire invoice is due within 30 days. Customers buying on credit create accounts receivable. The terms of these accounts can range from cash on delivery (C.O.D.) to due in 30, 45, 60 or 90 days from the date of delivery.

Segmentation and Targeting Strategy

Sell to Everyone

The first market segmentation strategy is the most broad: not defining a specific market. You attempt to sell to everyone. Although this sounds good and should result in the greatest sales, it is usually unrealistic. Because each group of consumers perceives their wants and needs differently, each one needs to be solicited with a specific message that will make this group remember and purchase your product. If a message is too general and vague, a broad range of consumers may see it, but no one group will remember and act on it.

Differentiated Marketing

The second approach to market segmentation is called differentiated marketing. It is the attempt to modify your product and marketing efforts in such a way that you solicit two or more segments simultaneously. The Levi's "501" promotions are an excellent example. By using various ethnic groups, younger age groups and both sexes in its commercials, Levi's solicits several specific markets individually, but all in the same advertisement.

Concentrated Marketing

The third and most limited segmentation strategy is called concentrated marketing. This is the selection of one, or only a few closely related target segments. For example, BMW targets young, upwardly mobile professionals in its TV commercials, which stress appearance, performance and prestige.

■ Distribution Channels

The final step in preparing your marketing plan is to decide how you will sell your product or service, where you are going to locate your business and how you are going to get your product or service to the customer. The purpose of the distribution process is to deliver what the customer wants to a place he will buy it. Several of the more common distribution channels are described in this section.

Direct Sales

Direct sales is the most common form of distribution. Examples of direct distribution companies are Avon, Firestone and Thom McAnn. Each produces its own product line, ships to regional warehouses (replacing the wholesaler) and then sells directly to consumers through its own retail outlets. The benefits of direct distribution are control over supply of raw materials, control of distribution and quality, increased buying power, lower administrative costs and ability to capture profits that would have been earned by other companies at the various stages of distribution.

Indirect Sales

Indirect sales strategies related to brand image include extensive, selective and exclusive distribution. Indirect distribution is where a manufacturer sells to a wholesaler who sells to a retailer who ultimately sells to the customer. The majority of firms operate at one level and do not control the entire distribution chain because of a lack of expertise and capital.

Variations of indirect distribution channels include OEMs (Original Equipment Manufacturers), Dealers and VARs (Value Added Retailers). In the early stages of a new product, when cash is tight, OEMs can generate and build new sales, while in the growth stage, Dealers and VARs are needed.

Extensive

Often described as the "shotgun" approach, extensive distribution sells your product or service through as many retailers as possible without regard to image or competition. This type of channel works best for convenience goods such as soap, pencils, film and other household goods. The idea is to sell through all responsible outlets where the customer would expect to find your product.

Selective

Selective distribution is the broad category between extensive and exclusive. You want to reach as many potential customers through as many responsible outlets as possible, but you want to maintain some type of image. This approach attempts to reach more than one customer profile or target market by selecting specific outlets with specific images and then matching product selection and promotion to that image. Good policy here includes avoiding outlets with bad credit, poor service, a bad customer image and a poor location. Selective distribution differs from extensive in that it subscribes to the concept that 80% of a company's sales come from 20% of its customers. There is no need to sell your product through every retail outlet under this distribution strategy.

Exclusive

Exclusive distribution, often called "the rifle approach," is selling your product or service at a very limited number of retail outlets, either a single store or chain. An example of this approach would be the Ralph Lauren apparel being sold in such department stores as Burdines and Lord & Taylors, but not Sears or J.C. Penney. The objective of exclusive distribution is to reach a single target market. It usually requires strong dealer loyalty and active sales support from the dealer. Exclusive distribution is "brand and image" conscious and is usually used in conjunction with a concentrated marketing strategy. In choosing this distribution strategy, it is important to avoid distributing to competing channels.

OEM

The OEM sale has the lowest marketing cost and the highest real margin. Wide market exposure and a solid market penetration is possible. An OEM will often "bundle" or promote its product with yours or pay a royalty on each product sold.

Dealers

Dealers add value to the product by providing floor space and end-user sales. Successful dealers prefer to buy from a distributor to minimize their vendor list. They want consolidated billing and dependable deliveries. Advertising and promoting your product will ensure dealer interest.

VARs

A VAR (Value Added Reseller) develops customer loyalty by "added value" to your product. A consultant is a good example of a VAR. A VAR does not make a product, but rather provides a service in addition to your product that is considered an extra value to the customer. A close and personal relationship along with training, referrals and regular communication help make VARs a good choice for channel distribution.

■ Advertising and Promotion

Doing business without advertising is like winking at a girl in the dark.
You know what you are doing, but nobody else does.

— Steuart H. Britt

Promotion

The goals of promotion are simple: to inform, to persuade and to remind.

Promotion includes advertising, publicity or public relations, personal selling and sales promotions. The promotional strategy you choose will be determined by marketing decisions you have already made. The purpose of a promotion is to tell potential customers that you have a product or service that can satisfy their demands, to convince those potential customers to buy from you and to successfully compete with other, similar businesses. Your message will depend on the target market you identify and how that market will perceive your message.

Advertising

Advertising is sending impersonal messages to selected large audiences for the purpose of soliciting or informing consumers. This includes such forms as television, radio, print, direct mail, outdoor billboards, signs on mass transit vehicles, point-of-purchase displays in stores and ads in the yellow pages. Which medium you choose is based on the target market and cost per person receiving the advertisement. In advertising, no individual representing your business is communicating directly with your potential customer. As a consequence, advertising messages are limited to one-way communications. Advertising works well when your target market strategy is to solicit business from a broad market. However, it can become quite specific when you choose local media such as newspapers, radio and television air time.

Sales Promotion

A sales promotion is marketing stimuli (messages) used to generate demand for your product or service. The purpose of a sales promotion is to convince those potential customers to buy from you immediately.

Examples of sales promotions targeted at consumers include special aisle displays, samples, coupons, contests, banners, and free gifts. Promotions are also aimed at wholesalers and internal salespeople and can include contests, sales aids, meetings, catalogs, price promotions, and trade shows.

Personal Selling

Personal selling is defined as a "person-to-person sales" presentation. The advantage of this approach is that it allows for two-way communication between your representative and your potential customer. Although personal selling generally results in more sales directly related to the promotional efforts, it is a very expensive form of promotion. Another disadvantage is that it can limit the size of your potential target market segment.

Some types of direct selling include the "canned" presentation where a sales representative recites a memorized sales pitch to the customer. Although this allows you more control over what message the customer receives, it does not allow for an open channel of communication such as the "feature versus benefit" approach, and often discourages potential customers. In feature versus benefit selling, your representative spends time asking the customer what his specific wants and needs are. He or she then attempts to show the customer how your business can satisfy those wants and needs better than any other competitor. This type of sales approach usually leaves the customer feeling satisfied with his decision. If there are any misunderstandings or reservations, your salesperson can handle them before closing the sale. Feature versus benefit direct selling is also an excellent opportunity for you to gain valuable insight into the wants and needs of your target market, to track changes in customer demand and to collect good feedback on performance.

Deciding which type of sales approach to choose determines what type of sales force you must hire. These decisions very closely follow your decision about distribution. You have the choice of hiring a captive direct sales force or using independent sales representatives who represent your company as well as other companies. If you choose independent representatives, your expenses will be lower, but you have less control over the representation of your company and products. If he or she is unprofessional or chooses to emphasize another product that will earn him a higher income, the sales and reputation of your business could suffer. With a captive direct sales force, you have increased expenses for employee salaries and benefits, such as Social Security, pensions, and medical insurance. Your choice of compensation includes salary, commission or some combination.

Personal selling is targeted directly at the final consumer, whereas advertising, publicity and public relations are aimed at a mass or large target audience.

Advertising Budget

How much to spend on advertising can be decided in a number of ways.

Marginal

The first method is the marginal approach and can be difficult to implement. The marginal approach is spending to the point where the last expenditure on advertising equals the net profit on sales generated by that advertisement (usually, large corporations use this approach).

Available Funds

A second method for determining how much to spend on advertising is the available funds approach, which is spending whatever you can afford. Although probably the most commonly used method, available funds is also the most conservative. The more you spend on effective advertising, the more sales you will generate. In other words, if you make the investment in quality advertising, you will generate the sales to pay for the advertising.

Budgetary

The next method to determine the amount to be spent on advertising is the budgetary approach—that is, spending a percentage of projected sales on advertising. If you want sales to reach a certain level next year, you need to spend a certain percentage on advertising during the year.

"Match dollar for dollar"

The final approach is to match "dollar for dollar" what your competition is spending. This method is based on the assumption that equal spending will at least keep you and the competition equal in terms of sales levels and market shares.

Cost of Advertising

To launch a new product into the market often requires a significant advertising budget. The cost of advertising your product is typically tied to forecasted sales, not past sales.

In deciding your advertising budget, the following guidelines are suggested.

- Trade shows (8%). They test consumer reaction to your product.
- Public Relations/Travel (5-8%). Most important area prior to a product's introduction.
- Collateral (3-8%). Highest percent of advertising dollars for product less than $100 and generally less for products more than $300.
- Direct Mail (33%). Spend a large percentage of your budget to generate end-user demand.
- End-User Catalog Sales (8%). Sales should offset your expenses; a good return would be two times the cost of advertising.
- Print Advertising, Trade/Channel (8%). Keep budget down; retailer will seek your product if they experience high end-user demand.
- Channel Promotions (26%). Distributors and resellers generally require a commitment to a promotional budget. Be creative and flexible.

Before choosing the appropriate advertising media, you should request a "media kit." This is an information packet with the demographics of the firm's readership or subscribers. These demographics should identify what type of customer reads that newspaper or magazine, listens to a certain radio station or watches that television channel. In addition, the media kit should describe what these consumers like to do and how they spend their money. You need to match your customer profile with the demographics of the advertising media in order to select the best one for your business.

Public Relations

Publicity is often referred to as Public Relations. Publicity is information about your product or company that is not a direct message from you to the potential customer. It is usually reported by an independent party. You do not directly pay for publicity, but its value to you in terms of sales can be dramatic. An example of publicity is the weekly food column in the newspaper. If you own a restaurant, you do not pay for a restaurant review, but information about your business, food and service is reported to the public. Publicity can be either good or bad, and you have little control over what is reported. The review that raves about the quality service at your restaurant can double sales overnight.

Major Sales Announcements

Major agreements should be written up and released to selected media as soon as possible after they are signed. Ideally, these would be joint announcements. At the same time, a shortened version of the release should be mailed to all internal and external sales organizations.

Press Releases

Prepare press releases on the entire product line/service area for each new product introduction, technical development, participation in a major event, awards/recognition for product/personnel excellence/performance, etc. Include an 8x10" black and white glossy photo of your product or an interesting demo of your service that editors will probably pick up at trade shows.

Use trade shows as another method for maintaining a high profile with the editors of key target media. If a major product announcement is feasible at a show, plan the announcement well in advance. However, since the major publications send their editors to the major shows, an opportunity exists to schedule short interviews between key personnel and selected reporters and editors. These mini-interviews can be used in lieu of the editorial visit (described below), or as opportunities to give editors a company or product update from a chief executive's point of view.

Editorial Visits

Inviting the most influential reporters and editors from targeted publications for a visit is important in maintaining high visibility in the marketplace. During the visit, each editor should receive a complete facility tour, product briefing and an opportunity to interview the chairman, president, product designer and marketing manager. If logistics or timing is a problem with the interviews, then these could possibly be arranged at the major trade shows.

Trade Shows

Trade shows are also a valuable way to evaluate the competition and to expand your knowledge of other products in your industry. The following factors should be taken into consideration when selecting which trade shows to attend:

- Target audience of the show; will this get the message to our target market?
- Geographic location; a good mix of shows around the country

- Time frame; preferably no more than one show each month
- Past experience, if any, with the show
- Participation in someone else's booth

A typical face-to-face sales call costs about $220 these days. At a trade show you enjoy having your full demo set up, all your brochures ready to go, your salespeople and managers are all there. . . and the prospects come to you! The trick is choosing which show to attend and planning to maximize your investment. The trade show media kit should include all the appropriate demographic and psychographic information–just like a magazine–so you calculate approximately how many of the right people might come by your booth. What's the cost of the lead, the value of being able to give them your full pitch right there, the value of your visibility at the show, etc.? Just make sure you have a plan to follow up on your prospects (don't laugh, a lot of companies lose it right here) or you're wasting your time and money right from the start.

List Management

List management is used to target your customers via a database containing names and addresses of your customer or potential customers. Customer lists can be purchased for target markets, but are more effective if developed in-house. Registration cards and periodic surveys will help you build your customer list and measure the success of your marketing activities by providing a historical profile of your customer.

Internal/External Newsletter

An internal or external newsletter serves as an informational piece for internal personnel, the sales force and key customers. It includes sections covering each major department or organization within the company, such as sales, marketing, manufacturing and R&D, as well as a message from the executive staff. It also highlights milestones such as key sales stories, successful customer applications, significant marketing events and product development news.

■ Marketing Plan Checklist

✓ How are you positioning your product and/or company?
✓ How are you determining the price for your product?
✓ Who are you planning to sell your product to?
✓ What type of distribution channel(s) do you plan to use?
✓ What type of advertising and promotion are you planning to use?
✓ How much money do you plan to spend on advertising and promotions?
✓ How can public relations be used in selling your product and/or company?

■ Review Questions

1. Why is price one of the most effective marketing tools? What should price be based on?

2. Your firm is manufacturing a highly technical item which had very high R&D costs. Your product was first to the market and still has very little competition. What price strategy would you recommend and why?

3. Your firm is manufacturing a gourmet fat-free line of salad dressings. What would you recommend for the distribution strategy–direct or indirect? Extensive or exclusive?

4. Tom Harlia is considering *Business Week* as a possible advertising medium for his luxury car import service. He calls the magazine to request its media kit. What information should he expect to receive?

5. How are public relations and publicity different from advertising? In what situations are public relations most beneficial?

6. Why do companies spend time and money attending trade shows as exhibitors of products or services?

■ Activities

1. Using the Marketing Plan worksheet (next page) or template (8-MKTPLN.DOC), describe the basic marketing plan, sales strategy and positioning strategy for your proposed venture.

2. Assume your company is making a phenomenal new after-market wiper blade for cars and trucks. The wiper material works better and lasts longer than anything on the market, but the car manufacturers are not interested in your product. Using the Distribution Channels section of the Marketing Plan worksheet or template, describe how you would distribute this product. Complete this section through the Returns and Adjustments Policy section.

3. Using the Advertising and Promotion section of the worksheet or template, describe the promotion strategy for your proposed product or service. (Stop at the Preliminary Media Schedule section.)

4. Contact a radio or TV station, a magazine, or a newspaper, and ask for a media kit including the Standard Rate and Data Sheet. How much might your proposed firm spend with this one media outlet in a one-year period?

8-MKTPLN.DOC

Marketing Plan

[*Company's*] _____ marketing strategy is to enhance, promote and support the fact that our products [*list your unique features, benefits, established market position/presence*] _____

_____

_____

The overall marketing plan for our product is based on the following fundamentals:

[*Type of business you want to be in*] _____

_____

[*Segment of the market(s) you plan to reach*] _____

_____

[*Distribution channel to be used to reach market segment: retail, jobbers, wholesalers, brokers, door to door, mail order, party plan, etc.*] _____

_____

_____

[*Share of the market we expect to capture versus time*] _____

_____

_____

To prove the value of [*product*] _____ we can _____

_____

_____

Sales Strategy

The target market segments to focus on are [*specific customers*] _____

_____

Because of [*product's*] _____ special market characteristics, [*seasonal/geographic/etc., as mentioned in Market Analysis*]

_____

our sales strategy [includes/incorporates] .... :

....

....

....

....

Positioning

Our [product, or similar/competition's product] ....

is seen by the consumer as [customer's perception of your product] ....

....

....

Its unique advantages [technical/quality/performance] ....

....

can be exploited to arrive at a winning position in the consumer's mind.

In terms of market segmentation advantages, we can use [upscale consumers/ethnic

appeal/etc.] ....

to arrive at a winning position here.

Pricing

The prices for our products are determined first and foremost by [competition/

costs/suppliers/manufacturers/package deals] ....

It is important to know that [sliding scales/volume/regulated/competitive/perceived

value] .... pricing is essential to our

market profile.

Compared to the competition, our prices are ....

Different seasonal aspects of our market affect our pricing because [example:

selling seasons] ....

....

We feel that our customers will pay $ .... because [purchasing rationale]

....

....

Margin Structure

Retail

....

....

Distributor

....

....

Manufacturer's Representative

....

....

Direct Sales

....

....

Discounts

We can take advantage of volume purchases by ....

....

....

....

We plan to review our pricing and product/service margin every _____months.

Current Selling Methods

We currently use [*activities used in selling your product or service*] ....

....

....

to sell [*product*] ....

Methods we use to promote [*product*] ....
include ....

....

....

Marketing Responsibilities

Responsibility for marketing and sales decisions lies with the following people in the company [*list name and title and area of responsibility*]:

....

....

....

....

Distribution Channels

[*Company's*] .... marketing department plans to sell our [*product*] ....through [*one or several channels*] .... The determining factors in choosing these channels are ....

....

....

Key competition uses the same [*or different*] .... distribution channels. Our mix of distribution channels will give us the advantages of [*list advantages*]

....

....

over our competition.

A partial list of [*Company's*] .... major current customers includes: ....

....

....

International Market

Our international strategy includes the following: ....

....

....

Method of Distribution

The primary means of distribution will be [*direct, executive sales, manufacturers' reps, distributors, retailers, OEMs, direct-response mail, telemarketing, and so on*] _____

_____

_____

Additional channels planned are _____

_____

Product Roll-out Program

For first entry into the market the specific market areas we have selected are [*list key roll-out market areas and activities*] _____

_____

After initial roll-out and evaluation of the results, we will expand our marketing to additional market areas in this order of priority: [*list additional market areas for intended penetration*] _____

_____

_____

Customer Service

Our customers emphasize that service and support is one of their major concerns. The following areas of support are available for our customers [*examples include toll-free hotline, free pickup and delivery, warehousing of customer inventory, technical backup to OEMs and manufacturers' reps*]: _____

_____

_____

Returns and Adjustments Policy

At this time, general trade customs for handling returns are [*describe how returns are generally handled*] _____

_____

We will use the following policies:

....

....

Advertising and Promotion

[*Company*] .... recognizes the key to success at this time requires extensive promotion. This must be done aggressively on a wide scale. To accomplish our sales goals, we require an extremely capable advertising agency and public relations firm. [*Company*] ....

[*plans to advertise/advertises in major trade magazines*] ....

such as .... Upon funding, an agency shall be selected and, with their assistance, a comprehensive advertising and promotion plan will be drafted. Advertising will be done independently and cooperatively with Distributors, OEM's, retailers and companies with whom

[*Company*] .... has joint marketing/sales relationships.

Objectives

Position [*Company*] .... as the leading

[*maker, servicer*] .... in the market.

Increase company awareness and brand name recognition among business managers and .... retailers, buyers, customers.

Generate qualified sales leads and potential new distributors for field sales organization.

Develop, through market research, significant information to create immediate and long-term marketing plans.

Create product advertising programs supporting the [*better taste, lower fat, more fun*] .... position.

Coordinate sales literature, demonstration materials, telemarketing programs and direct response promotions in order to ....

....

Advertising Campaign

The best way to reach our potential customers is to develop an intense advertising campaign promoting our basic premise—[your selling basis, theme, position in market] " _____

_____ ."

To [maintain/establish] _____ our _____ company image, the delivery and tone of our statements will be [understated elegance, hard-driving excitement, excellence, glamour, reality, slice-of-life]

_____ .

Ads will convey the look and feel of a [describe your image] _____

_____

company.

Research indicates that [direct mail, direct response, TV, radio, certain publications] _____

_____

is the best media outlet for advertising our product.

To eliminate the biggest objections to immediate action, our advertisements must address [known/anticipated objections, difficulties with product acceptance, how to own/use product immediately] _____ .

Preliminary Media Schedule

[Make a chart like this one for each publication and other outlet.]

	Circulation	Budget	Ad Size
[Magazine, TV, Radio] _____	50,000	$1,500	1/4 Page
_____	450,000	$4,400	1/2 Page
Total _____	500,000	$5,900	3/4 page

Anticipated Response: _____ responses at $_____ each.

We expect to achieve a reach of [total circulation/audience] _____ , and to maintain that for a period of at least [months] _____ .

Due to the [seasonal, geographical, etc.] _____ nature of

our audience, we plan to [*how you will counter these issues*] _____
_____
_____ .

In regard to competitors' advertising, it is necessary to _____
_____ .

Promotion

In addition to standard advertising practices, we will gain considerable

recognition through [*trade shows, press releases, various promotions, consumer incentives,*

direct mail] _____
_____
_____ .

Advertising Budget

For the next _____ [*months/years*] _____ advertising and

promotion will require $ [*figure about 10 to 20% of sales the first year*] _____ .

On an ongoing basis we will budget our advertising investment as _____ % of

total sales.

This figure is necessary because of [*the specific goals you must meet*] _____
_____
_____ .

Public Relations

Our publicity efforts are intended to accomplish the following:

Position [*Company*] _____ at the leading edge in

providing [*product for industry or market segment*] _____ .

Increase [*Company*] _____ reputation and [*name/brand*]

_____ recognition among [*managers/buyers/customers in*

prospective companies/industries/markets] _____ .

Communicate on a regular basis with three target publics:

[*Editors of major trade, business and local publications*] _____
_____ .

[*Key management personnel in the existing customer companies*] ....

[*Organization of employees and sales reps*] ....

Publicity Strategy

During 19........... [*Company*] .... will focus on the following publicity strategies:

Develop a sustained public relations effort, with ongoing contact between key editors and top-level personnel including plan/facility visitations.

Develop a regular and consistent product update program for the major target media, keeping key editors abreast of .... enhancements and .... new product introductions.

Develop an internal newsletter that can cover key sales successes, significant marketing and manufacturing events, technical support and product development stories. Internally, the newsletter would be targeted at all company personnel and sales reps; externally the piece would be targeted at key customers and prospects.

Develop a minimum of .... technical articles written by key executives or engineers to be placed in [*list publications*] ...., ... and .... within the next .... months.

Establish contact with editorial staff for the purpose of being included in product "round-ups"—product comparisons in [*publications such as Consumer Reports*] ...., where competing products are compared. This exposure builds credibility and market acceptance.

Produce a complete company backgrounder on [*Company*] .... to be used as the primary public relations tool for all target media editorial contact. This will also be effective for inclusion in press kits, dealer kits and sales packages.

*I never did anything worth doing by accident,
nor did any of my inventions come by accident;
they came by work.*

— Thomas Edison

Part 3: Completing Your Financial Plan

The financial portion of your business plan is a narrative that presents summaries of your business' financial history (if applicable), your financial projections and the assumptions you based them on, your projected capital requirements and how the capital will be used, and your plan to repay your lenders and/or investors. Before you can write your financial plan narrative, you need to generate a set of projected financial statements that reflect the goals and information you've provided in the previous sections of your business plan.

This section covers:

- The Purpose of a Financial Plan
- Financial Statement Overviews
- Projecting Financial Statements
- Using the Financial Plan Spreadsheets
- The Financial Statements

- Printing the Financial Statements
- Customizing the Financial Statements
- Financial Plan Checklist
- Financial Plan Narrative Text
- Financial Plan Worksheet

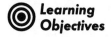 *Learning Objectives*

After completing Part 3, you should be able to:

1. Understand the function of your financial plan

2. Know the various components in common financial statements

3. Project financial statements for your company

4. Determine capital requirements for your firm's start-up, expansion or reorganization

■ The Purpose of a Financial Plan

Your projected financial statements are the tools you will use to determine if your business is viable, and if so, what capital you will require to proceed. The financial statements model the financial operation of your business in the same way that you might model a production process or inventory flow. When used to forecast your business' capital requirements, these statements are often referred to as financial projections or pro forma statements. When completed, these projected financial statements should be included in the Supporting Documents section of your business plan, along with your historical financial statements, if applicable.

Although you are probably not an accountant, it is important that you understand some basic goals and principles of accounting and some of the methods and statements accountants use for recording financial information. The more you understand about financial statements, how to project them, and how to analyze them, the more reasonable and valuable your projected statements will be. As a result, the financial plan portion of your business plan will be more thorough, which may assist you in obtaining financing.

The following section assumes you understand some basic accounting principles, the most common financial statements and several financial analysis methods. You may need to review a basic introductory accounting textbook. If you have additional or specific accounting questions, we suggest you consult your accountant.

■ Financial Statement Overviews

This section discusses the function of each of the most common financial statements, and the key components in each statement.

What Are Financial Statements?

Basically, financial statements are standardized forms developed by accountants and financial managers to record business transactions. Financial statements are designed to reflect standard accounting practices and follow a fundamental principle of accounting: matching costs and expenses with the revenues they created. In order for costs and expenses to be matched with revenues, accountants devised what is known as the double entry system of accounting.

What are the Financial Statements Templates?

BizPlan*Express* includes a set of financial spreadsheet templates to help you produce financial statements in support of your business plan. Using your spreadsheet processor, you edit the templates with your own financial data.

- In BizPlan*Express*, you can use the individual Basic spreadsheets. If you have a large number of spreadsheets to create, you may want to consider investing in BizPlan*Builder* in order to use the Integrated Financials, where all of the spreadsheets are tied together.

Although we've provided a selection of financial statements, you may not need or want to include all of them in your business or marketing plan. Only prepare and include the financial statements that are appropriate for your needs.

Gross Profit Analysis Statement

The Gross Profit Analysis statement presents a breakdown of the month-by-month sales, cost of goods sold and gross profit for each product or product line. It can assist you in determining the profitability of individual products and how they contribute to your total gross profit. This statement is most appropriate for multi-product businesses, but it can often be adapted for use by mixed product/service and service-only businesses.

Budget Statement

The Budget Statement presents a month-by-month projection of revenues and expenses over a one-year period. Your budget is the foundation for projecting your other financial statements. It presents a more detailed accounting of your expenses than on your Income Statement. On a budget, expense details are usually grouped by department or functional area, such as General and Administrative.

Income Statement

The Income Statement, also known as a Statement of Operations, or a Profit & Loss or P & L Statement, summarizes your revenue and expense projections on a monthly basis for one year, or an annual basis for several years. Like your budget, it presents your sales, cost of goods sold, gross profit, operating expenses (by category totals only, such as Sales and Marketing, General and Administrative, and Research and Development), income from operations, other income and expenses, income taxes and net income. You should calculate year one income statement for each month, and then calculate three to five years of annual statements.

The budget is primarily used as an internal document that details all of your expenses for departmental and management review and approval. The income statement is normally used in place of the budget within a business plan, and whenever financial statements are issued to potential lenders and investors. When you review issues such as operating expenses with people outside your company, the income statement format helps focus the discussion on the reasonableness of category expenses in total (such as General and Administrative), instead of individual expenses (such as Postage or Telephone).

Cash Flows Statement

The Cash Flows Statement, also known as a Statement of Changes in Financial Position, summarizes your cash-related activities on a monthly basis for one year, or an annual basis for several years. Basically, cash flows statements show where your cash came from and where it went. The format of a cash flows statement can vary, but it often begins with the net income from your budget or income statement, then shows adjustments for items that do not involve cash (such as payables and depreciation); other non-operational sources and applications of cash are listed next (such as fixed asset purchases and financing proceeds and payments), then the net cash balance is calculated.

Balance Sheet

The Balance Sheet, also known as a Statement of Financial Position, shows the financial position of your business at the end of a period, such as the end of a month or the end of a year. The income statement shows your sales revenue and related expenses for a time period resulting in your net income (or loss) for the period, which then becomes the increase (or decrease) in equity in your balance sheet. The balance sheet represents a "snapshot" of your company's resulting financial position, encompassing everything your company owns (Assets), owes (Liabilities) and the equity of the owner(s). The balances are a snapshot because they reflect your position on a specific day, not what has occurred over a period of time.

The balance sheet is divided into two parts which must always equal each other:

Assets = Liabilities + Equity

Assets

Assets are those items your company owns. On a balance sheet, assets are commonly grouped into Current Assets, Fixed Assets and Other Assets categories.

Current Assets: These are cash and other assets that are expected to be turned into cash or consumed within one year. These include investments; accounts receivable and notes; inventory (including raw materials, work in process and finished goods); and other current assets. Other current assets include prepaid expenses, such as insurance premiums or advertising costs that must be paid in advance but are "used up" over a period of time.

Fixed Assets: Also called Plant and Equipment, these are assets which are of a durable nature and are expected to help generate revenue over a period of a year or longer. Fixed assets can include equipment, automobiles, furniture and fixtures, land, and buildings. They are listed at cost on the balance sheet and are depreciated over a period of years. Depreciation is recorded as an expense in the budget, and to an account called accumulated depreciation on the balance sheet, which acts as a reduction to the total value of the fixed assets.

Other Assets: This asset category may include such accounts as patents, copyrights or goodwill.

On the other side of the balance sheet are liabilities and equity.

Liabilities

Liabilities are those accounts or debts that your business owes others, and they are commonly grouped into Current Liabilities and Long Term Debt.

Current Liabilities: These are debts that are expected to be repaid within a year, including short term debt payable to the bank (including the portion of long term debt due within one year); accounts payable to suppliers for materials, supplies, etc.; other payables for items like payroll taxes or sales taxes; and accrued liabilities (such as bonuses or pension plans that are paid in the future but relate to performance over the current or prior fiscal period).

Long Term Debt: These are those loans from a bank or other lenders that are due to be repaid over a period of a year or longer. Usually, these loans are mortgages or were used to purchase fixed assets.

Equity

The final category on the balance sheet is equity. Although the exact listing of accounts is determined by what type of business you own (i.e., a proprietorship, partnership or corporation), the equity category summarizes the accumulated wealth of your company. This includes capital, which is the amount that has been invested into your company, retained earnings, which are the accumulated profits (or losses) the company has earned from operations less dividends declared, and dividends payable, which are dividends that have been declared but not yet paid to the shareholders. Equity is the value that is left after you've subtracted your total liabilities from your total assets.

Beginning Balance Sheet Balances

As soon as you spend or invest your first dollar, you have a financial position that can be presented on a balance sheet. The equity section would reflect your personal investment, as well as any money invested from other sources. Assets may have been purchased, liabilities may have been incurred, and expenses have probably been incurred.

Since a balance sheet reflects your cumulative financial position through a certain day, all activity that occurs prior to your first budget month must be added to the new activity for that month to accurately project your balance sheet as of the end of the first budget month. Because of this, you will need to calculate what your beginning balance sheet balances are (what your balance sheet would show on the day before you start your budget period), so that these beginning balance sheet amounts can be incorporated into your projections.

Break-Even Analysis Statement

The Break-Even Analysis Statement can assist you in predicting the effect of changes in costs and sales levels on the profitability of your business. This statement is usually used as an internal tool to test the sensitivity of your sales projections and the effects of management decisions regarding expenditures. The format of a break-even analysis statement can vary; one common monthly format uses the budget as its foundation, but separates all expenses into fixed or variable categories. Then it calculates the Contribution Margin, Break-Even Sales Volume and Sales Volume Above Break-Even for each month of your budget year.

> **Note:** Costs or expenses are considered variable in nature if they vary directly with changes in sales volume, such as material and labor costs. Costs or expenses are considered fixed if they stay about the same as sales volume changes, such as rent or Vice President salaries.

■ Projecting Financial Statements

Whether you are researching a business proposal, starting a new business or expanding an existing business, there are two main reasons why you'll want to prepare projected financial statements. The first is to determine if your proposed business venture, expansion or project can be successful, and the second is to set goals and to chart a financial course for your business to follow in the future. For either purpose, you will need to research the probable expenses of the venture and the market sales potential, and then quantify the results of this research in your projected financial statements.

Be Conservative

When projecting your financial statements, you should follow the accounting principle of conservatism. Conservatism states that if there is a choice of values, the more conservative value must be chosen: the lower value for an asset or revenue item, the higher value for an expense or debt. One of the first things potential lenders or investors will be looking at is reasonableness; in other words, are the numbers you've projected possible? Lenders and investors may form an impression of you as an individual based on how reasonable they think your projected financial statements are. If they get the impression that you're the type of person who embellishes a lot, they may begin to question all of your financial projections, as well as other parts of your business plan.

Remember, projected financial statements do not stand on their own. They must be supported by research on your market that indicates your business or venture can be successful. Do not manipulate the numbers in your projected financial statements to indicate the possibility of success if the research in your written business plan does not support those numbers!

Consider Multiple Projection Scenarios

You may want to prepare not only one set of projections, but three. They should include a pessimistic (worst case) scenario, an optimistic (best case) scenario and a realistic (most likely) scenario. In this way, you will have a true picture of your potential for gain and loss. While the best case is what you hope for, the worst case is what you need to be prepared for; in the meantime, the most likely case will be the basis for many of your decisions.

How Much Money Do I Need?

In order to estimate your capital requirements, you will need to consider each of the potential uses for the financing funds, including (but not limited to): research and development, fixed asset purchases and working capital. As you analyze each, you'll need to project how much money you'll need, when you'll need it, and what type of financing is most appropriate for each.

Financing Research and Development

You may need funds to finance research and development (R & D) activities in order to turn a product concept into a prototype, and a prototype into a final product. Frequently, there is a long delay between the time money is paid out for R & D expenses and the time sales and profits are generated as a result of the efforts. Because of this, it may be appropriate to fund your R & D activities with long term financing.

Financing Fixed Asset Purchases

You may need funds to finance fixed asset purchases, such as new equipment to produce a new product, or a larger manufacturing facility to increase your production capacity. As for R & D expenses, there is often a long delay between the time money is paid out for fixed assets purchases and the time sales and profits are generated as a result of the new assets. Also, the dollar values of fixed asset purchases can be very large. For these reasons, fixed asset purchases are almost always funded with long term financing.

Financing Working Capital

Working capital is the cash that allows a business to operate, stock inventory and carry accounts receivable before collecting the money from customers. The financing requirement for working capital is "permanent" and grows proportionally with growth in sales volume. Growth consumes a lot of cash. Many people overlook the fact that if your sales increase 50%, your working capital requirements may also increase about 50%. In other words, if you have $200,000 in working capital and sales increase 50%, you may need an additional $100,000 in working capital. Frequently, short term debt can be arranged using your accounts receivable and inventory as collateral; however, this is not always the best approach. If you repeatedly need to borrow money to fund working capital, it may be more appropriate to obtain long term financing, if possible.

Your cash flows statement can assist you in determining how much money you need by anticipating your actual cash requirements. Once you've projected how much money you think you will need to finance each of these areas and when, incorporate these estimates into your cash flows statements in the appropriate time periods. Then, review your cash flows statements and look for large cash balances or shortfalls; you may need to adjust the amounts of your financing requirements or the timing of those requirements.

Once you've refined your financing projections, add the amounts you've projected for each financing use, then estimate an additional percentage over that sum to use as your total financing requirement; a general guideline to follow is to raise 50% more capital than your projections indicate you'll need.

■ Using the Financial Plan Spreadsheets

Note: We assume that you are already familiar with operating your spreadsheet program. If you have never used your spreadsheet processor, we strongly recommend that you work through the tutorial lesson(s) *before* attempting to use any of the BizPlan*Express* spreadsheet templates. See Appendix A for instructions about installing and using the spreadsheet files.

The financial spreadsheets included in BizPlan*Express* are standard, pre-formatted spreadsheet files. Within these spreadsheets, generic financial statements/analyses have been constructed using labels and formulas in many of the spreadsheet cells; other cells are formatted to accept the values you enter.

These generic financial statements provide the structure for presenting a professional level of financial detail using standard accounting formats and terms. By providing this structure, the BizPlan*Express* spreadsheets can help simplify the task of projecting financial statements for your business.

The particular set of financial statements you need will vary depending on the nature of your business and your purpose for writing a business plan. However, you will generally want to include at least a Budget, Balance Sheet and projected Income Statement. Additionally, you may want to include Cash Flows Statements (also known as Statements of Changes in Financial Position) and analyses such as Gross Profit and Break-Even.

Getting Started with the Spreadsheets

Follow these general steps to complete your financial statements:

1. **Install the spreadsheet files**. If you haven't installed the spreadsheet files onto your hard disk, follow the instructions in Appendix A. Then, open the file you want to use.

2. **Enter your values into the spreadsheet(s)**. Enter your estimated values into each spreadsheet you need. Replace the sample values with your values.

3. **Recalculate the spreadsheet(s)**. When you have finished entering your estimated values, be sure each spreadsheet recalculates.

   After the spreadsheet is recalculated, some cells may display ########## or **********. See Displaying Large Dollar Values below.

4. **Review your financial statements**. Review the financial statements, either on screen or by printing drafts. Your projections should be conservative and realistic, and you should have assumed sufficient financing to maintain a positive cash balance. Refine your financial statements as needed.

5. **Print your completed financial statements**.

6. **Summarize your financial projections**. Analyze your completed financial statements. Summarize your financial projections in the Financial Plan word processing template (see Financial Plan Narrative Text, page 107).

■ The Financial Statements

This section describes the financial statements you can prepare with BizPlan*Express*. Each financial statement is in a separate spreadsheet. **We suggest you work on the statements in the order presented, skipping any statements that you don't need or want to include in your plan.** The spreadsheets are delivered with sample values entered into some of the line items. You can replace the sample values with your own values as you work your way down through the line items in the spreadsheet. If you prefer, you can "zero out" the spreadsheet in preparation for entering your estimated values by replacing the sample values with zeros and recalculating the spreadsheet.

Displaying Large Dollar Values

*After the spreadsheets have been recalculated, some cells may display ########## or * * * * * * * * * *. This indicates that the value in the cell is too large for the column width. Set the column width to at least 5 characters more than the number of digits in the value (this allows for dollar signs, commas and parentheses). For example, to display ten million dollars (which has 8 digits), your column width should be at least 13.*

Some spreadsheet processors will not allow you to set the column width in a protected spreadsheet. Refer to your documentation to learn how to disable protection for a spreadsheet.

Note: Some spreadsheet processors, including Lotus 1-2-3 for Windows, refer to a protected spreadsheet as Sealed rather than Protected.

Gross Profit Analysis by Product/Service (Year 1 by month)

The Gross Profit Analysis presents a month-by-month projection of revenues and costs of goods sold by sales item for the first budget year. This analysis calculates the monthly gross profit for each sales item by subtracting the monthly costs for Material, Labor, and Fixed Cost of Goods & Services for each item from the monthly sales for each item.

*** GROSS PROFIT ANALYSIS by Product/Service (Year 1 by month) ***

	Jul - 95	Aug - 95	Sep - 95	Oct - 96	Nov - 96	Dec - 96	Year 1	% of Sales
Product/Service A:								**% of Sales**
Sales	$20,000	$20,000	$20,000	$20,000	$20,000	$20,000	$280,000	
Material	$5,500	$5,500	$5,500	$5,500	$5,500	$5,500	$77,000	27.50%
Labor	$2,000	$2,000	$2,000	$2,000	$2,000	$2,000	$28,000	10.00%
Fixed Cost of Goods & Services	$2,535	$2,567	$2,599	$2,632	$2,666	$2,700	$30,239	10.80%
Gross Profit	$9,965	$9,933	$9,901	$9,868	$9,834	$9,800	$144,761	51.70%
% of Sales	49.83%	49.67%	49.51%	49.34%	49.17%	49.00%	51.70%	
Product/Service B:								**% of Sales**
Sales	$2,145	$2,170	$2,195	$2,221	$2,247	$2,273	$25,607	
Material	$644	$651	$659	$666	$674	$682	$7,683	30.00%
Labor	$107	$109	$110	$111	$112	$114	$1,281	5.00%
Fixed Cost of Goods & Services	$181	$183	$186	$188	$190	$193	$2,160	8.44%
Gross Profit	$1,213	$1,227	$1,240	$1,256	$1,271	$1,284	$14,483	56.56%
% of Sales	56.55%	56.54%	56.49%	56.55%	56.56%	56.49%	56.56%	
Product/Service C:								**% of Sales**
Sales	$8,000	$8,500	$9,000	$9,500	$10,000	$10,500	$93,000	
Material	$800	$850	$900	$950	$1,000	$1,050	$9,300	10.00%
Labor	$3,200	$3,400	$3,600	$3,800	$4,000	$4,200	$37,200	40.00%
Fixed Cost of Goods & Services	$905	$917	$928	$940	$952	$964	$10,800	11.61%
Gross Profit	$3,095	$3,333	$3,572	$3,810	$4,048	$4,286	$35,700	38.39%
% of Sales	38.69%	39.21%	39.69%	40.11%	40.48%	40.82%	38.39%	
Product/Service D:								**% of Sales**
Sales	$0	$0	$0	$0	$0	$0	$0	
Material	$0	$0	$0	$0	$0	$0	$0	0.00%
Labor	$0	$0	$0	$0	$0	$0	$0	0.00%
Fixed Cost of Goods & Services	$0	$0	$0	$0	$0	$0	$0	0.00%
Gross Profit	$0	$0	$0	$0	$0	$0	$0	0.00%
% of Sales	0.00%	0.00%	0.00%	0.00%	0.00%	0.00%	0.00%	
Product/Service E:								**% of Sales**
Sales	$0	$0	$0	$0	$0	$0	$0	
Material	$0	$0	$0	$0	$0	$0	$0	0.00%
Labor	$0	$0	$0	$0	$0	$0	$0	0.00%
Fixed Cost of Goods & Services	$0	$0	$0	$0	$0	$0	$0	0.00%
Gross Profit	$0	$0	$0	$0	$0	$0	$0	0.00%
% of Sales	0.00%	0.00%	0.00%	0.00%	0.00%	0.00%	0.00%	
Product/Service F:								**% of Sales**
Sales	$0	$0	$0	$0	$0	$0	$0	
Material	$0	$0	$0	$0	$0	$0	$0	0.00%
Labor	$0	$0	$0	$0	$0	$0	$0	0.00%
Fixed Cost of Goods & Services	$0	$0	$0	$0	$0	$0	$0	0.00%
Gross Profit	$0	$0	$0	$0	$0	$0	$0	0.00%
% of Sales	0.00%	0.00%	0.00%	0.00%	0.00%	0.00%	0.00%	
Product/Service G:								**% of Sales**
Sales	$0	$0	$0	$0	$0	$0	$0	
Material	$0	$0	$0	$0	$0	$0	$0	0.00%
Labor	$0	$0	$0	$0	$0	$0	$0	0.00%
Fixed Cost of Goods & Services	$0	$0	$0	$0	$0	$0	$0	0.00%
Gross Profit	$0	$0	$0	$0	$0	$0	$0	0.00%
% of Sales	0.00%	0.00%	0.00%	0.00%	0.00%	0.00%	0.00%	
Product/Service H:								**% of Sales**
Sales	$0	$0	$0	$0	$0	$0	$0	
Material	$0	$0	$0	$0	$0	$0	$0	0.00%
Labor	$0	$0	$0	$0	$0	$0	$0	0.00%
Fixed Cost of Goods & Services	$0	$0	$0	$0	$0	$0	$0	0.00%
Gross Profit	$0	$0	$0	$0	$0	$0	$0	0.00%
% of Sales	0.00%	0.00%	0.00%	0.00%	0.00%	0.00%	0.00%	

File: BUDGET.XLS

Budget (Year 1 by month)

The Budget statement presents a month-by-month projection of revenues, cost of goods sold, and detailed operating expenses for the first budget year. This statement calculates the percentage of Total Sales each sales item represents, and the total monthly and annual amounts for Sales, Gross Profit, Income From Operations, and Net Income After Taxes, as well as monthly and annual totals for each operating expense category.

If you have a multi-product business and you have completed the Gross Profit Analysis statement, reenter the sales values from the Gross Profit Analysis into the Budget. Also, add the cost of goods sold values for each product (from the Gross Profit Analysis) and enter the resulting totals into the cost of goods sold line items on the Budget. Then, enter your estimated values for the other line items that are appropriate to your circumstances.

For information on adding, renaming or deleting items from the Budget, see Customizing the Financial Statements, page 102.

*** BUDGET (Year 1 by month) ***

	Jul - 95	Aug - 95	Sep - 95	Oct - 96	Nov - 96	Dec - 96	Year 1	% of Total Sales
Sales								
Product/Service A-Product	$20,000	$20,000	$20,000	$20,000	$20,000	$20,000	$280,000	70.24%
Product/Service B-Parts	$2,145	$2,170	$2,195	$2,221	$2,247	$2,273	$25,607	6.42%
Product/Service C-Service	$8,000	$8,500	$9,000	$9,500	$10,000	$10,500	$93,000	23.33%
Product/Service D	$0	$0	$0	$0	$0	$0	$0	0.00%
Product/Service E	$0	$0	$0	$0	$0	$0	$0	0.00%
Product/Service F	$0	$0	$0	$0	$0	$0	$0	0.00%
Product/Service G	$0	$0	$0	$0	$0	$0	$0	0.00%
Product/Service H	$0	$0	$0	$0	$0	$0	$0	0.00%
Total Sales	$30,145	$30,670	$31,195	$31,721	$32,247	$32,773	$398,607	100.00%
Cost of Goods Sold								
Material	$6,944	$7,001	$7,059	$7,116	$7,174	$7,232	$93,983	23.58%
Labor	$5,307	$5,509	$5,710	$5,911	$6,112	$6,314	$66,481	16.68%
Total Variable COGS	$12,251	$12,510	$12,769	$13,027	$13,286	$13,546	$160,464	40.26%
% of Total Sales	40.64%	40.79%	40.93%	41.07%	41.20%	41.33%	40.26%	
Fixed Cost of Goods & Services								
Production Management Salaries	$1,048	$1,056	$1,064	$1,072	$1,081	$1,090	$12,531	3.14%
Production Facility Expense	$2,145	$2,170	$2,195	$2,221	$2,247	$2,273	$25,607	6.42%
Production Equipment Rental	$0	$0	$0	$0	$0	$0	$0	0.00%
Small Tools / Supplies	$210	$220	$230	$240	$250	$260	$2,460	0.62%
Packaging Supplies	$218	$221	$224	$227	$230	$234	$2,599	0.65%
Other Production Expenses	$0	$0	$0	$0	$0	$0	$0	0.00%
Total Fixed Cost of Goods & Services	$3,621	$3,667	$3,713	$3,760	$3,808	$3,857	$43,197	10.84%
% of Total Sales	12.01%	11.96%	11.90%	11.85%	11.81%	11.77%	10.84%	
Total Cost of Goods Sold	$15,872	$16,177	$16,482	$16,787	$17,094	$17,403	$203,661	51.09%
Gross Profit	$14,273	$14,493	$14,713	$14,934	$15,153	$15,370	$194,946	48.91%
% of Total Sales	47.35%	47.25%	47.16%	47.08%	46.99%	46.90%	48.91%	
Operating Expenses								
Sales & Marketing								
Advertising	$800	$850	$900	$950	$1,000	$1,050	$9,300	2.33%
Commissions	$452	$460	$468	$476	$484	$492	$5,980	1.50%
Entertainment	$192	$199	$206	$213	$220	$227	$2,262	0.57%
Literature	$450	$475	$500	$525	$550	$575	$5,250	1.32%
Promotions	$0	$0	$0	$0	$0	$0	$0	0.00%
Salaries	$559	$569	$580	$591	$602	$613	$6,659	1.67%
Trade Shows	$0	$0	$0	$0	$0	$0	$0	0.00%
Travel	$260	$270	$280	$290	$300	$310	$3,060	0.77%
Total Sales & Marketing Costs	$2,713	$2,823	$2,934	$3,045	$3,156	$3,267	$32,511	8.16%
% of Total Sales	9.00%	9.20%	9.41%	9.60%	9.79%	9.97%	8.16%	

File: INCOME1.XLS

Income Statement (Year 1 by month)

The Income Statement presents a month-by-month projection of revenues, cost of goods sold, and summarized operating expenses for the first budget year. This statement calculates the percentage of Total Sales each sales item represents, and the total monthly and annual amounts for Sales, Gross Profit, Income From Operations, and Net Income After Taxes, as well as annual totals for each operating expense category.

The Income Statement (Year 1 by month) is identical to the Budget except that operating expenses are summarized by category on the Income Statement, while on the Budget the operating expenses are shown in detail. It may be easier for you to project your expenses in detail on the Budget, but you may prefer the summarized format of the Income Statement for presentation in your business plan. If so, reenter the appropriate values from your Budget into the Income Statement (Year 1 by month), and include only the Income Statement in the Supporting Documents section of your business plan.

File: CASHFLW1.XLS

Cash Flows (Statement of Changes in Financial Position: Year 1 by month)

The Cash Flows (Year 1 by month) statement, also called a Statement of Changes in Financial Position, presents a monthly projection of your sources of cash and your applications of cash for the first budget year. This statement calculates the monthly net increase or decrease in Cash, and annual totals for each cash source and application.

The values for the Net Income After Taxes and Depreciation line items on the monthly Cash Flows statement should be reentered from the corresponding lines on your Budget. You will need to estimate values for the other operational Sources of Cash, such as Accounts Payable and Accounts Receivable, based on the revenues and expenses you've projected on your Budget and the time delays you expect in making and receiving payments. Then, enter your estimated values for the other line items that are appropriate to your circumstances.

In general, enter all amounts as positive values; the exception is for operational sources of cash, such as Accounts Payable. If the source of cash has increased during the month, enter the amount as a positive value; if the source of cash has decreased during the month, enter the amount as a negative value.

Once you've entered all of your estimated Cash Flows values, review the resulting values calculated on the Ending Cash Balance line. If the ending cash balance is negative for any month, you may need to revise your Financing estimates to project additional cash proceeds from either loans or the sale of stock. After you've revised your estimates, recalculate the spreadsheet and check your ending cash balances again; repeat this process until your projected cash balances are positive.

*** CASH FLOWS (STATEMENT of CHANGES in FINANCIAL POSITION: Year 1 by month) ***							
Sources of Cash:	Jul - 95	Aug - 95	Sep - 95	Oct - 96	Nov - 96	Dec - 96	Year 1
Operations during the year:							
Net Income After Taxes	$1,327	$1,321	$1,313	$1,305	$1,294	$1,283	$37,827
Add items not decreasing cash							
Depreciation	$83	$83	$83	$83	$83	$83	$996
Increase in Accounts Payable	($5,996)	$254	$254	$254	$256	$258	$14,503
Increase in Other Payables	$0	$0	$0	$0	$0	$0	$0
Increase in Accrued Liabilities	$0	$0	$0	$0	$0	$0	$0
Deduct items not increasing cash							
Increase in Accounts Receivable	($23,950)	($18,950)	$1,050	$1,051	$1,052	$1,052	$65,020
Increase in Inventory	($8,780)	$1,220	$1,223	$1,228	$615	$618	$64,612
Cash from Operations	$28,144	$19,388	($623)	($637)	($34)	($46)	($76,306)
Financing & Other:							
Sale of Stock	$0	$0	$0	$0	$0	$0	$0
Proceeds from Short Term Loans	$0	$0	$0	$0	$0	$0	$0
Proceeds from Long Term Loans	$0	$0	$0	$0	$0	$0	$100,000
Sale of Investments	$0	$0	$0	$0	$0	$0	$0
Collection of Notes Receivable	$0	$0	$0	$0	$0	$0	$0
Reduction of Other Current Assets	$0	$0	$0	$0	$0	$0	$0
Reduction of Other Assets	$0	$0	$0	$0	$0	$0	$0
Cash from Operations & Financing	$28,144	$19,388	($623)	($637)	($34)	($46)	$23,694
Applications of Cash:							
Payment of Dividends	$0	$0	$0	$0	$0	$0	$0
Purchases of Fixed Assets	$0	$0	$0	$0	$0	$0	$0
Repayment of Short Term Loans	$0	$0	$0	$0	$0	$0	$0
Repayment of Long Term Loans	$0	$0	$0	$0	$0	$0	$0
Purchase of Investments	$0	$0	$0	$0	$0	$0	$0
Increase in Notes Receivable	$0	$0	$0	$0	$0	$0	$0
Increase in Other Current Assets	$0	$0	$0	$0	$0	$0	$0
Increase in Other Assets	$0	$0	$0	$0	$0	$0	$0
Increase/(Decrease) in Cash	$28,144	$19,388	($623)	($637)	($34)	($46)	$23,694
Change in Cash Balance							
Beginning Cash Balance	$17,502	$45,646	$65,034	$64,411	$63,774	$63,740	$40,000
Increase/(Decrease) in Cash	$28,144	$19,388	($623)	($637)	($34)	($46)	$23,694
Ending Cash Balance	$45,646	$65,034	$64,411	$63,774	$63,740	$63,694	$63,694

File: BALANCE1.XLS

Balance Sheet (Year 1 by month)

The Balance Sheet (Year 1 by month) statement presents a projection of your financial position at the end of each month of the first budget year. This encompasses everything a company owns (Assets), owes (Liabilities) and the equity of the owner(s).

The monthly values in the Balance Sheet are **cumulative**; this means that they reflect the previous month's values plus (or minus) any activity from the current month to project a "snapshot" of your position at the end of each month. To complete the Balance Sheet, combine the Balance Sheet values for the previous month with the activity for the current month (from the Cash Flows statement) and enter the result into the current month on the Balance Sheet. For example, Retained Earnings for the sixth month would be projected as the sum of Retained Earnings for the fifth month (from the Balance Sheet) plus Net Income After Taxes for the sixth month (from the Cash Flows statement).

The exception to this is for Cash; since the cumulative Ending Cash Balances have already been calculated on the Cash Flow statement, these values can simply be reentered on the Cash line item in your Balance Sheet.

A completed Balance Sheet must be in balance; specifically, **Total Assets must equal Total Liabilities & Equity**. If you include a Balance Sheet as a Supporting Document to your business plan, be sure that it is in balance!

*** BALANCE SHEET (Year 1 by month) ***								
As of the Month Ending:								
Assets	Jan - 95	Feb - 95	Mar - 95	Apr - 95	May - 95	Jun - 95	Jul - 95	Aug - 95
Current Assets								
Cash	$82,605	$49,362	$25,337	$8,362	$6,182	$17,502	$45,646	$65,034
Investments	$0	$0	$0	$0	$0	$0	$0	$0
Accounts Receivable	$17,000	$39,523	$50,570	$66,618	$92,666	$103,715	$79,765	$60,815
Notes Receivable	$0	$0	$0	$0	$0	$0	$0	$0
Inventory	$49,909	$61,121	$77,336	$88,552	$84,769	$73,488	$64,708	$65,928
Other Current Assets	$0	$0	$0	$0	$0	$0	$0	$0
Total Current Assets	$149,514	$150,006	$153,243	$163,532	$183,617	$194,705	$190,119	$191,777
Plant & Equipment								
Land	$0	$0	$0	$0	$0	$0	$0	$0
Buildings	$0	$0	$0	$0	$0	$0	$0	$0
Building/Leasehold Improvements	$0	$0	$0	$0	$0	$0	$0	$0
Machinery & Equipment	$10,000	$10,000	$10,000	$10,000	$10,000	$10,000	$10,000	$10,000
Office Equipment	$0	$0	$0	$0	$0	$0	$0	$0
Automobiles	$0	$0	$0	$0	$0	$0	$0	$0
Less Accumulated Depreciation	($583)	($666)	($749)	($832)	($915)	($998)	($1,081)	($1,164)
Total Net Plant & Equipment	$9,417	$9,334	$9,251	$9,168	$9,085	$9,002	$8,919	$8,836
Other Assets	$0	$0	$0	$0	$0	$0	$0	$0
Total Assets	$158,931	$159,340	$162,494	$172,700	$192,702	$203,707	$199,038	$200,613
Liabilities & Owners' Equity								
Current Liabilities								
Short Term Debt	$0	$0	$0	$0	$0	$0	$0	$0
Accounts Payable	$8,583	$10,398	$12,213	$15,591	$20,532	$19,223	$13,227	$13,481
Other Payables	$0	$0	$0	$0	$0	$0	$0	$0
Accrued Liabilities	$0	$0	$0	$0	$0	$0	$0	$0
Total Current Liabilities	$8,583	$10,398	$12,213	$15,591	$20,532	$19,223	$13,227	$13,481
Long Term Debt	$100,000	$100,000	$100,000	$100,000	$100,000	$100,000	$100,000	$100,000
Total Liabilities	$108,583	$110,398	$112,213	$115,591	$120,532	$119,223	$113,227	$113,481
Owner/Stockholder Equity								
Common Stock	$60,000	$60,000	$60,000	$60,000	$60,000	$60,000	$60,000	$60,000
Retained Earnings	($9,652)	($11,058)	($9,719)	($2,891)	$12,170	$24,484	$25,811	$27,132
Less Dividends Payable	$0	$0	$0	$0	$0	$0	$0	$0
Total Owners' Equity	$50,348	$48,942	$50,281	$57,109	$72,170	$84,484	$85,811	$87,132
Total Liabilities & Equity	$158,931	$159,340	$162,494	$172,700	$192,702	$203,707	$199,038	$200,613

Financial Statements (Years 1 – 5)

File: INCOME5.XLS

File: CASHFLW5.XLS

File: BALANCE5.XLS

The spreadsheets in this package include annual statements (years 1-5) for the Income Statement, Cash Flows, and Balance Sheet. The examples are not shown here but have the same rows as the monthly examples.

File: BREAKEVN.XLS

Break-Even Analysis (Year 1 by month)

The Break-Even Analysis presents a month-by-month summarized projection of revenues, fixed costs, and variable costs for the first budget year, and calculates the monthly Contribution Margin, Break-Even Sales Volume, and Sales Volume Above Break-Even for both Income from Operations and Net Income After Taxes. This statement is usually used as an internal tool to anticipate the effect that sales volume increases or decreases will have on your income stream.

Reenter the values for this analysis from the corresponding line items on your Budget. (Combine the values for Interest Income and Interest Expense from the Budget, and enter the net result on the Interest Income (Expense) – Fixed line on the Break-Even.)

You may elect to reclassify some fixed costs as variable costs for the purpose of analyzing break-even margins. If so, be sure that you enter your estimated amounts in the Less Reclassified Fixed Costs line as negative values, then enter the same amounts as positive values in the Plus Reclassified Fixed Costs line.

*** BREAK-EVEN ANALYSIS (Year 1 by month) ***								% of Total
	Jul - 95	Aug - 95	Sep - 95	Oct - 96	Nov - 96	Dec - 96	Year 1	Sales
Sales	$30,145	$30,670	$31,195	$31,721	$32,247	$32,773	$398,607	
Fixed Costs								
Fixed Cost of Goods & Services	$3,621	$3,667	$3,713	$3,760	$3,808	$3,857	$43,197	10.84%
Sales & Marketing (w/o Commissions)	$2,261	$2,363	$2,466	$2,569	$2,672	$2,775	$26,531	6.66%
Research & Development	$3,685	$3,743	$3,801	$3,860	$3,919	$3,979	$43,915	11.02%
G & A (w/o Depreciation)	$5,529	$5,606	$5,684	$5,762	$5,841	$5,920	$65,920	16.54%
Depreciation	$83	$83	$83	$83	$83	$83	$996	0.25%
Less Reclassified Fixed Costs	$0	$0	$0	$0	$0	$0	$0	0.00%
Total Fixed Costs	$15,179	$15,462	$15,747	$16,034	$16,323	$16,614	$180,559	45.30%
Variable Costs								
Material and Labor	$12,251	$12,510	$12,769	$13,027	$13,286	$13,546	$160,464	40.26%
Commissions	$452	$460	$468	$476	$484	$492	$5,980	1.50%
Plus Reclassified Fixed Costs	$0	$0	$0	$0	$0	$0	$0	0.00%
Total Variable Costs	$12,703	$12,970	$13,237	$13,503	$13,770	$14,038	$166,444	41.76%
Income from Operations	$2,263	$2,238	$2,211	$2,184	$2,154	$2,121	$51,604	12.95%
Interest Income (Expense) - "Fixed"	($788)	($770)	($752)	($734)	($716)	($698)	($9,574)	-2.40%
Income Taxes - "Variable"	$148	$147	$146	$145	$144	$140	$4,203	1.05%
Net Income After Taxes	$1,327	$1,321	$1,313	$1,305	$1,294	$1,283	$37,827	9.49%
Income from Operations Analysis								
Contribution Margin	57.86%	57.71%	57.57%	57.43%	57.30%	57.17%	58.24%	
Break-Even Sales Volume	$26,234	$26,792	$27,354	$27,918	$28,488	$29,063	$310,007	77.77%
Sales Volume Above Break-Even	$3,911	$3,878	$3,841	$3,803	$3,759	$3,710	$88,600	22.23%
Net Income After Taxes Analysis								
Contribution Margin	57.37%	57.23%	57.10%	56.97%	56.85%	56.74%	57.19%	
Break-Even Sales Volume	$25,085	$25,671	$26,261	$26,854	$27,452	$28,051	$298,981	75.01%
Sales Volume Above Break-Even	$5,060	$4,999	$4,934	$4,867	$4,795	$4,722	$99,626	24.99%

■ Printing the Financial Statements

Although printing is a function of your specific spreadsheet program and your specific printer, the following are a few general guidelines that may assist you with printing the BizPlan*Express* financial statements. For more information on printing options, refer to your spreadsheet processor's manual or on-line help, or the manual for your printer.

1. **Save the spreadsheet before issuing a print command**. This protects your work in the event that your system locks up while attempting to execute the print command. Use the "Save As" comand and give the spreadsheet a new name. That way you'll still have the original document as well.

2. **Set the printer/page setup options for the spreadsheet or range**. For example, if you have selected the Cash Flows Statement you'll probably want to print on letter-size paper with a portrait (vertical) orientation and a standard font size, since the statement is only six columns wide. If you have selected the Budget, you'll probably want to print on either letter- or legal-size paper with a landscape (horizontal) orientation and a small (condensed) font size (if your printer can support these options), since the Budget is fifteen columns wide. How you set your printer/page setup options depends on your spreadsheet processor and your printer.

3. **Print the spreadsheet or selected range**.

Repeat these steps for each statement you want to print.

■ Customizing the Financial Statements

The BizPlan*Express* spreadsheet can help simplify the task of projecting financial statements for your business. The generic financial statements provide a professional level of financial detail using standard accounting formats and terms.

Although the spreadsheets were designed to meet the needs of a variety of businesses, we recognize that there may be situations that require customization of some of the financial statements, especially the Budget. While we can't be held responsible for the integrity of any customized spreadsheets, we do want to provide you with some guidelines to help you successfully customize the spreadsheet to meet your needs. These guidelines address the common customization needs of previous BizPlan*Express* users.

> **Note:** In this discussion, "customizations" refers to overwriting labels and formulas in locked (protected) cells, not to inputting sales item labels or estimated values in the provided cells.

Do not attempt to customize the BizPlan*Express* spreadsheets unless you are an experienced spreadsheet user! You can irreparably damage the integrity of the spreadsheets by editing or deleting certain cells.

General Customization Guidelines

Refer to your spreadsheet program reference guide for customization guidelines. These general guidelines may be useful as well.

1. **Save your spreadsheet file *twice* before you begin any customization work**. To minimize the customizations you'll need to make, be sure you've entered your assumptions or estimated values and fine-tuned them as needed until the calculated results are as close as possible to an accurate projection of your business' position. Then, save the spreadsheet once under a different file name (as a backup in case you change your mind or make an error), and once under the file name you've been using.

2. **Unprotect the spreadsheet file**. See the Cell Protection box on the next page.

3. **Make your customizations**. In general, the spreadsheets were designed so that changes to a cell affect cells to the right of and below the changed cell; cells to the left of and above a changed cell are usually not affected. Because of this structure, it is best to *work on one row at a time across (left to right) and down in the spreadsheet*.

4. **Refer to How Do I...? for specific guidelines**. The How Do I...? section on the next page provides suggestions on making customizations for several specific situations. Check this section to see if your situation (or one close to it) is discussed.

5. **Reprotect the spreadsheet file**. Once you've completed your customizations, we strongly recommend that you reprotect the spreadsheet file so cells cannot be overwritten by accident.

Spreadsheet Protection

The BizPlan*Express* spreadsheets are delivered with some cells formatted as locked (protected), and with protection enabled for the spreadsheet itself. This was done to prevent formulas and important labels from being overwritten by accident, which could irreparably damage the integrity of the spreadsheet.

If you try to edit a locked cell when protection is enabled for the spreadsheet file, your spreadsheet processor will disallow the edit and give you a message that the cell is locked (protected). Therefore, you will need to disable the protection for the spreadsheet file before you can perform any customizations. Refer to the reference manual (or on-line help) for your spreadsheet processor for information on how to disable protection for a spreadsheet.

Note: Some spreadsheets, including Lotus 1-2-3 for Windows, refer to a protected spreadsheet as Sealed rather than protected.

6. **Review the spreadsheet, and resave the file**. Recalculate the spreadsheet file, then scroll through it and review the results of your customizations. Make sure that an error condition has not been created as a result of a change you made, and "manually" spot-check a few of the totals to ensure the logic of the formulas is still intact. If everything appears correct, resave the spreadsheet file. **We strongly recommend that you keep the uncustomized backup file** (the one you saved under a different file name before you made the customizations) in case you discover an error later on. This can help you avoid having to "start over from scratch."

How Do I...?

This section has tips for handling some of the customization issues previous BizPlan*Express* users have encountered.

How do I rename a Budget expense item?

You may want to rename one or more of the expense items on the Budget that you don't need in order to "add" item(s) that you do need (or to clarify the name of an item).

To rename an expense item, locate the row for the expense item in the Budget, then replace the sample name by entering the name you want in column A. Make sure that the "new" item belongs in the same category as the item you are replacing. (In other words, don't replace a General & Administrative item with the name of a Research & Development item.)

How do I add rows for more Budget items?

You may want to add one or more rows to the Budget to accommodate additional item(s). If so, you can customize the spreadsheet file to add rows directly to the Budget statement. However, adding rows can jeopardize the integrity of the spreadsheet and the accuracy of the financial statements. For this reason, **we strongly recommend that you consider renaming items instead** (as discussed above), and/or consolidating values for several related items to use only one row of the Budget.

To add a row, locate the line in the Budget where you'd like the new row to appear, position your cursor in that row, then use the appropriate command for your spreadsheet processor to insert a new row. Make sure that the item you are adding the new row for belongs in the category where you've added the row. (In other words, don't add a row in the General & Administrative section if you need a new line for a Research & Development item.)

Once you've added a new row, you'll need to enter your label for the item in column A and your monthly values in columns C through N. You'll also need to create or copy formulas for the annual total in column O and the percentage in column P. (Remember to reformat the cells in the new row if they don't match the formatting of the other rows.) Finally, verify that the values you enter on the new row are being included in the total for that category.

How do I delete rows for unused Budget items?

You may want to delete the rows that contain items that don't apply to your circumstances (for example, unused sales items, expense items or balance sheet items).

Before you make decisions on which rows to omit from your printouts, keep in mind that **including an item with zero values lets anyone who reviews your business plan know that you considered the item and deliberately set it to zero**. A "missing" (omitted) item may cause a reviewer to think you overlooked the item. This is especially true for expense, cash flow and balance sheet items.

To delete a row, locate the row that you'd like to eliminate from the statement, position your cursor in that row, then use the appropriate command for your spreadsheet processor to delete a row. **Make sure that the row you are deleting is not a totaling row**. (Once you've deleted a row, you should verify that the total for that category is still being calculated correctly.) Also, if the item you deleted appears on another statement (such as sales items, which appear on the Budget and the Income Statements), you will probably want to delete it from the other statement as well for consistency.

■ Financial Plan Checklist

✓ Have you done the background research necessary to prepare your financial statements: operating expenses, sales projections, etc.?

✓ Have you prepared three sets of financial projections (best case, worst case, most likely case)?

✓ Have you completed the appropriate projected financial statement worksheets for your business?

✓ Have you carefully analyzed each financial statement, and do you understand the significance of the numbers you're projecting?

✓ Do you know how much capital you need and when you need it? Have you determined what types of financing are appropriate?

✓ Can you explain in detail how you plan to use any financing you receive?

✓ Have you determined an exit/payback strategy for lenders and investors?

✓ Have you summarized your financial position in a written Financial Plan, which is part of your business plan? See page 108.

✓ Have you consulted your financial advisor or a business analyst for assistance when needed?

✓ Have you included projected and historical financial statements in the Supporting Documents section of your plan? See page 113.

■ Review Questions

1. What is meant by "pro forma" financial statements?

2. Why are costs of goods sold broken down into two categories – fixed costs and variable costs (labor and materials)?

3. What is the income statement? How does it differ from the budget statement?

4. What is the balance sheet?

5. When should you conduct a break-even analysis? What does the contribution margin represent?

6. Why should you follow the principle of conservatism when projecting your financial statements?

7. What is ratio analysis and how is it used?

8. What is working capital? Why is it so critical to the health of your business?

■ Activities

1. A small business that manufactures specialty bottles for perfume has four products (A, B, C and D). Using the following information and the template for Gross Profit Analysis by Product/Service, calculate the gross profit and percent of sales for the next three months.

Product Sales	Material Costs as a % of sales	Labor Costs as a % of sales
A: $42,000	24%	20%
B: $97,000	11%	17%
C: $26,000	19%	20%
D: $38,000	15%	15%

Fixed costs are $50,000 per month, distributed to the four products depending upon their percentage of total sales. For example, product A will get $10,350 of the $50,000 since sales for A are approximately 20.7 % of total sales for the business. Sales are forecast to increase 1% the second month, and the third month will see a 5% increase over the second month.

2. Using the figures from activity number 1 and the template for the budget, calculate a budget for the three months. Use the following information to complete your budget.

Information is per month:

Production Mgmt Salaries	$18,000.00
Production Facility Expense	$22,000.00
Equipment Rental and Leases	$6,500.00
Small Tools/Supplies	$2,000.00
Packaging Supplies	$1,500.00

Advertising	$8,000.00
Commissions	$30,450.00
Entertainment	$200.00
Literature	$500.00
Trade Shows	$1,000.00
Travel	$4,000.00

Consulting	$700.00
R&D Materials	$300.00
R&D Salary	$2,500.00

Accounting	$500.00
Admin Salaries	$3,800.00
Depreciation - office equip	$100.00
Insurance	$2,000.00
Office Expenses	$500.00
Office Rental	$500.00
Taxes - Non-Income	$100.00
Telephone	$500.00
Utilities	$500.00

Interest Expense	$2,500.00
Taxes on income	10%

3. Using the information from the previous two activities, calculate the income statement using the Income Statement template in the book.

4. Using the Cash Flows (Statement of Changes in Financial Position) template, the following information, and information from the previous exercises (such as net income), calculate the changes in cash balance for the next three months.

Increases in Accounts Payable for months 1-3: $3,000	$1,500; $1,500;
Increases in Accounts Receivable for months 1-3: $20,000	$10,000; $10,000;
Increases in Inventory for months 1-3: $6,000	$3,000; $3,000;
Increase in Accrued Liabilities:	$6,000 only in the 3rd month
Repayment of long term loans:	$2,000; $2,000; $2,000
Purchase of used forklift:	$12,000 in the 2nd month
Beginning cash balance:	$27,000

Income figure for the first month is the net income for Month 1 that you calculated in #3.

5. Using the following information and the Balance Sheet template in this section, create a balance sheet for the company for the first month only.

Cash	$27,000
Accounts Receivable	$230,000.00
Inventory	$113,000.00
Machinery and Equipment	$200,000.00
Office Equipment	$14,000.00
Accumulated Depreciation	$25,200.00
Accounts Payable	$30,000.00
Accrued Liabilities	$40,000.00
Long Term Debt	$200,000.00
Common Stock	$100,000.00
Retained Earnings	$218,800.00

6. For each of the four products detailed in the previous activities, calculate a Month 1 break-even analysis using the text template. Distribute the fixed costs based on the percentage of sales method used in activity 1. Commissions are 15% of sales. Income taxes are 10%. Distribute the $100 of monthly depreciation on office equipment as $25 to each product.

■ Financial Plan Narrative Text

The written Financial Plan portion of your business plan should be brief and direct and should summarize your financial position. This is where you "go for the close," summarizing your business plan presentation and asking for the cash.

The financial plan does not include your projected financial statements, historical financial statements (if applicable) or financial analyses. These should be included with other relevant information in the Supporting Documents section of your business plan. Exactly what you say in your Financial Plan is dependent on your type of business, your target audience for your business plan and your purpose for writing a business plan.

Keep in mind that projected financial statements do not stand on their own. Anyone reviewing your financial statements will also expect to read a discussion that supports the projections you made (research on market, competition, etc.).

If you are using your business plan to apply for a loan or solicit investors, you need to target your statements to the interests and concerns of your potential lenders and investors. The basic question to ask yourself when writing the Financial Plan section of your business plan is: "What would I want to know to evaluate a business proposal before I would consider investing my own money?" If you have answered all the questions that you would have as an investor, you are probably prepared for lenders or outside investors.

The financial plan overview at the beginning of Part 3 has some information that can give you some perspective on what lenders and investors will be looking for in your business plan. Consult your financial advisor if you need additional assistance to complete your Financial Plan narrative.

File: 9-FINPLN.DOC

Assumptions

The financial projections are based on the assumption that the additional [*equipment/facility/product lines*] ....

will generate an increase in profits of [$/%] .... within .... [*years/ months*]. The new equipment will reduce costs by $..............., thereby increasing our profit margin by ....%.

Cost of Goods Sold will be reduced by ....% by taking advantage of volume discounts.

We plan to have a working prototype by [*month*]..................................... 19........ . Field testing of the product is to start by [*month*]..................... 19........ and be completed by [*month*]..................... 19........ . Initial market penetration is anticipated to be $............ at a margin of ....%, and increase to $............ at the end of the first year and $............ by the end of the fifth year.

General inflation rates are assumed to be ....% per year.

Summary/Analysis of Financial Statements

(a) Calculate the growth percents over prior years by taking each year's amount minus the previous year's amount, then dividing by the previous year's amount.

(b) You need to manually calculate any ratios you plan to include.

The following table highlights the primary income-related items:

Year	19____	19____	19____	19____	19____
Sales	$	$	$	$	$
% Growth (a)		%	%	%	%
Gross Profit Dollars	$	$	$	$	$
% Growth (a)		%	%	%	%
Operating Income Dollars	$	$	$	$	$
% Growth (a)		%	%	%	%
Net Income Dollars	$	$	$	$	$
% Growth (a)	$	$	$	$	$
Income Ratios: (b)					
Year	19____	19____	19____	19____	19____
Gross Profit Margin	%	%	%	%	%
Operating Income Margin	%	%	%	%	%
Net Income Margin	%	%	%	%	%
Return on Equity	%	%	%	%	%

Gross Profit Analysis

The Gross Profit Analysis in the Supporting Documents section shows monthly sales revenue, cost of goods sold and gross profit values for each of our product lines for the first year.

Income Statement

The Income Statement in the Supporting Documents section shows annual values for five years.

Balance Sheets

There are two Balance Sheets in the Supporting Documents section. One reflects the first year by month, and the second shows annual values for five years.

Break-Even Analysis

The Break-Even Analysis in the Supporting Documents section indicates that the break-even point will be reached in [month]_____ 19____. Sales are projected to be $_____ above break-even in [month]_____ 19____. The contribution margin for the first year is _____% representing $_____.

Cash Flows Statements

There are two Statements of Changes in Financial Position (Cash Flows Statements) in the Supporting Documents section. One reflects the first year by month, and the second shows annual values for five years.

Capital Requirements

The [initial/first year/total] _____ capital required is $_____.
We require additional investments of $_____, $_____, $_____ and $_____ in [years/months] _____, [years/months] _____, [years/months] _____ and [years/months] _____, respectively, to enable us to increase our production capacities to meet market demand.

After analyzing our working capital, we estimate our operating working capital requirements as $_____, $_____, $_____, $_____ and $_____ for years one through five, respectively. We will need to borrow $_____ to finance working capital for a period of [years/months] _____, the remainder to be financed through cash from operations.

In order to purchase [additional facilities/equipment/inventory] _____
_____, an estimated total of $_____ loan financing is required for the five-year period. The annual requirements for each year are estimated as $_____, $_____, $_____, $_____ and $_____ respectively.

The level of safety is [normal/low/high] _____ for this [industry/type of investment]_____. Our confidence in achieving the attached financial projections within _____% is [high/average/90%]_____. In addition to the operation of the business, additional protection is provided by _____ as collateral. In a [worst case/liquidation/unforeseen] _____
_____ situation, the realizable value of the collateral would be $_____, reducing the amount "at risk" to $_____. With a projected return of $_____, this represents a return of _____% of the amount "at risk."

How Funds Will Be Used

The [loan/equity investment] _____ proceeds will be used

to [purchase/buy/build/develop/gain/acquire/finance] _____

[equipment/facilities/working capital] _____ .

Exit/Payback Strategy

The financial projections indicate that exit of [investor] _____

will be achievable in _____ years. The exit settlement will be in the form of

_____ .

The increase in profits generated by _____

will allow us to have the funds to repay the loan in _____ [months/years].

Conclusion

Based on the attached financial projections, we believe that this venture
represents a sound business investment.

In order to [start/continue/proceed] _____ , we are

requesting a [loan/investment] _____ of $ _____ by

[date] _____ , 19 _____ .

> *A man can succeed at almost anything for which he has unlimited enthusiasm.*
>
> — *Charles M. Schwab*

Part 4: Executing Your Plan

Part 4 explains how to work with your finished business plan. There are three main sections:

- **Supporting Documents** lists a variety of additional documents you might include to substantiate your business plan, such as company brochures and resumes of key individuals. Page 113.

- **Presenting Your Plan** details how to assemble, print and distribute your plan. Page 114.

- **Funding Your Plan** details dozens of different methods and sources for securing funding. Page 120.

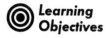 **Learning Objectives**

After completing Part 4, you should be able to:

1. Suggest a list of additional documents you might include to substantiate your business plan

2. Review, assemble and print your business plan to ensure a professional appearance

3. Describe the purpose of various items that may be included with the business plan, such as a cover letter, non-disclosure agreement, and clause that prohibits copying or further distribution

4. Realize there are dozens of different methods and sources for securing financing, and determine which ones are most appropriate for your situation

Chance favors the prepared mind.

— Louis Pasteur

Supporting Documents

Your supporting documents include information that supports the major points in the business plan—the items used to develop your plan. Include items that are too extensive to be included in your business plan, but will assist the reader in understanding the background of your plan and the basis of your rationale and projections.

Your may include some or all of the following documents:

- Organization chart and list of job responsibilities
- Resumes of key people
- Product specifications, photographs, brochures, drawings
- Letter from patent attorney stating likelihood of patent application being accepted
- Price Schedule for product line or service
- Floor plan for retailer or manufacturer
- Equipment in inventory
- Market analysis data
- Samples of advertising copy or publicity articles
- Personal financial statements, tax returns and credit reports of owners
- Copies of contractual agreements
- Commitment letters from major customers, suppliers, and lenders
- References (either letters or contact points) from lawyers, accountants, suppliers and banks

Financial Statements

- Gross Profit Analysis
- 12 Month Budget
- 12 Month Income Statement
- 12 Month Cash Flows
- 12 Month Balance Sheet
- 5 Year Income Statement
- 5 Year Cash Flows
- 5 Year Balance Sheet
- Break-Even Analysis

(See Part 3, Completing Your Financial Plan, for instructions about preparing your financial statements.)

Life affords no higher pleasure than that of surmounting difficulties, passing from one step of success to another, forming new wishes and seeing them gratified.

— Samuel Johnson

Presenting Your Plan

Your target audience will judge your company by the presentation of your business plan. It should be clearly and concisely written, informative and verifiable. Your plan must be presented and packaged in an effective and professional manner. This section covers many useful suggestions in these areas.

This section includes:

- Reviewing Your Plan
- Packaging Your Plan
- Making Your Presentation
- Following Up with Your Readers
- Checklist for Presenting Your Plan
- Non-Disclosure Agreement Worksheet

■ Reviewing Your Plan

Remember, your reader may typically spend only five to ten minutes reviewing your business plan. The Executive Summary and Financials sections must especially encourage the reader to read the other sections of your business plan. Review the following questions. Does your plan address these important questions?

- Have I conveyed my company's vision?
- Do I have the needed management team in place?
- Is there a market for my product or service?
- Have I given a clear description of my product or service?
- Have I defined my target market?
- Do I understand my competitors' weaknesses and strengths?
- Are the Financials realistic and in line with lending patterns?
- Does the plan describe the ROI for the investor?

If your company is well portrayed in your business plan, then distribute your plan and see what the reaction is. If the plan achieves your intended purpose immediately, we congratulate you!

You have now created a document that is easy and simple to update as needed. If adjustments in plans for your business are recommended, and you agree with their recommendations, make the necessary changes and try again. Some of the biggest success stories have come from people who received numerous rejections along the way. Use the recommendations to learn and apply what is necessary, and your next business plan will set you on the course to success.

■ Packaging Your Plan

Your business plan may vary in length depending on the product or service and the intended purpose of the plan. In most cases, limit the plan to anywhere from five to 35 pages, not including Financials and other supporting documents.

After you've completed the first draft of your business plan, be sure to check the plan for spelling, grammar and punctuation. Solicit someone with editing skills to review the plan for both content and grammar. Errors can easily turn off a potential investor or other evaluator.

The final version of your plan should be typed or printed on a laser output printer. Use high quality paper for the final copy. A 20-pound bond paper or better in white, ivory or gray creates a professional appearance.

To ensure a professional appearance, limit your document to two or three fonts. Enhance the key points with bold, italic or underline. Standard, easily readable type such as Helvectica for titles and Times Roman or Palatino for the body of the text is recommended. Frame your text by leaving a margin of at least 1 inch around the top, bottom, left, and right margin. Don't be afraid to leave white space as this will make your plan easier to read.

The use of plastic spiral (GBC) binding or covers purchased at an office supply store will also provide a professional look. If your plan is going to bankers or investors, it helps if you can find a way to stand out from the crowd. Show some creativity by dressing up the cover to reflect something about your business.

Before distributing your business plan, have your lawyer, accountant and other professionals review and approve or sign off on the sections they helped prepare. You should number each plan and have a place for the signature of those to whom you are circulating the plan. This conveys the value of the plan and helps protect its proprietary nature. If appropriate, include a private placement disclaimer on the first sheet. It is also a good idea to include a personalized cover letter to each person to whom you send the plan, highlighting his or her particular interests.

Distribution

Now that you have your business plan written and printed, you are ready to distribute it. Limit access to those individuals who are either potential investors or who may have significant impact on your business.

For tracking, number the plans and list the name of the individuals who have received the copy. Use a number below 12 to indicate that the number of individual copies of the plan is limited. If you release different versions of the document, you may want to add a code to the number (example: Copy 12C).

Prohibit copying by including a statement on the Title Page or Table of Contents, such as:

"The contents of this plan are proprietary and confidential. It is not to be copied or duplicated in any way."

It is important to place a disclaimer on your title page to indicate that your plan is not an offering for sale but rather a document for informational purposes. Consult an attorney for a recommendation on the appropriate disclaimer. An example of a typical disclaimer might be:

"This is a business plan. It does not imply an offering of Securities."

Mailing out unsolicited business plans violates securities laws when the plan contains language offering to sell stock in your company. The only exception to this rule would be Rule 504, Private Placements, which does permit general solicitations. Do not mail out unsolicited plans or advertise for investors unless you qualify for the Rule 504 exemption.

If you are not sure, take the precaution of establishing a business or personal relationship with a prospective investor before you send them anything. Offers to family, friends, and business associates are rarely considered solicitation.*

Finally, insist that a Non-Disclosure Agreement be signed by each reader. This is a simple statement in which readers agree to refrain from revealing the plan's contents or ideas to anyone else. See the Non-Disclosure Agreement template on page 119.

■ Making Your Presentation

If you are using your plan to raise capital, you may want to personally present it to bankers or investors. Many of the same rules of writing a business plan apply to presenting it.

Keep it short and to the point. For instance, limit your presentation to half an hour or less. Like your written plan, the presentation should be concise and easy to understand. Extract the most important points (see the Executive Summary in Part 2) and run through them in an interesting and logical way. Don't be afraid to be enthusiastic about your product or service, but be realistic in your claims. Use visual aids. Using slides or overheads with simple points or phrases helps to keep your audience focused.

Involve several members of your management team. For example, have your marketing executive speak for five minutes and then have your financial executive review the highlights of his or her area. This will give your audience exposure to your team.

If appropriate, demonstrate your product or service. Bring a sample, if possible. Generating enthusiasm and excitement for your product or service is the best way to gain the confidence of the banker or investor. Leave a written copy of your business plan so the banker or investor can review information that may not have been covered by your presentation.

Non-Disclosure Agreement

This agreement is designed to protect your company, ideas, assets and competitive position from inappropriate use of your confidential information by

---

* *Source: Heather Anderson, Attorney (Denver, Colorado), Data Merge Financial News Release, #4.*

the evaluator of your business plan. Keep the agreement short, and make sure that it provides you with clear and adequate protection.

Cover Letter

When submitting a business plan, it is essential that you include a cover letter. The cover letter is the first document read, so keep it brief. At the same time, you want to motivate the reader to continue reading your business plan.

The cover letter should include name of your company and type of business; reason you have chosen this person to receive your plan; vision and mission of your company, in brief; intended purpose of submitting your business plan for evaluation; amount and type of funding you are seeking, if applicable; allocation/use of the funding, and return on investment for investor.

File: COVERLTR.DOC

You can use the BizPlan*Express* template COVERLTR.DOC to create your cover letter.

■ Following Up with Your Readers

Having completed and distributed the business plan, it is time to follow up with your potential investors and other readers. Approximately seven to ten days after you have delivered your business plan, follow up with a brief and professional phone call or letter to confirm that the evaluator has received your plan. Determine their reaction to your business plan and identify your next steps. See Funding Your Plan later in Part 4 and Appendix B, Resources, for additional resource material.

■ Congratulations!

You have spent much time and effort developing your business from a concept into something real. You have also spent a considerable amount of time going through the process of writing a business plan.

Your plan will not only communicate what your business is about, but will assist you in getting a better handle on your business and help build a foundation for business success. Congratulations on taking this next big step for your business and yourself.

■ Presenting Your Plan Checklist

✓ Have you checked the spelling, grammar, and punctuation?

✓ Has someone who has experience with other business plans or your business reviewed your plan?

✓ Have you checked the page numbers in the Table of Contents?

✓ Have you taken steps to give your plan a professional appearance:

- Have you typed the plan or printed it on a laser output printer?

- Have you used 20-pound bond paper or better in white, ivory or gray?

- Have you limited the plan to two or three typefaces? Helvetica for titles and Times Roman or Palatino for the body of the text are recommended. Have you enhanced key points with bold, italic or underline? Don't overdo the highlighting!

- Have you left at least a one-inch margin at the top, bottom, and sides of the page?

- Have you included index tabs to separate the sections of the plan?

- Have you bound the business plan with GBC binding?

- Have you numbered the title page of each copy?

✓ Have your lawyer, accountant and other professionals reviewed and signed off on the sections they helped prepare?

✓ Have you written a personalized cover letter to each person to whom you are sending the plan?

✓ Have you included a non-disclosure agreement? If you're using the agreement that's in this book, has your attorney reviewed and approved it?

■ Review Questions

1. Why should supporting documents, such as resumes of key personnel, be included with your business plan?

2. Why should someone other than you check the plan before printing?

3. Why should your business plan include a disclaimer that it is not implying an offering of securities?

4. What are some important points to keep in mind as you present your business plan?

5. What is a Non-Disclosure Agreement? Why is it important?

6. What should the cover letter include?

■ Activities

1. List the supporting documents that would be applicable to your business plan.

2. Assume you are approaching a local bank for a $125,000 loan to expand your current business, Thrift 'n Swift, a printing company that caters to small businesses. Write a cover letter to introduce your business plan for the expansion of this business.

3. The sample non-disclosure agreement in the text is geared toward a potential investor such as a venture capital firm. Assume you are handing your business plan to a potential key employee, a person you hope will join you as Vice President of Marketing in return for a small salary and some stock options...with the potential of striking it rich when the company goes public in about five years. Modify the non-disclosure agreement to fit this situation.

NONDISCL.DOC

The undersigned acknowledges that [Company] _____ has furnished to the undersigned potential Investor ("Investor") certain proprietary data ("Confidential Information") relating to the business affairs and operations of [Company] _____ for study and evaluation by Investor for possibly investing in [Company] _____.

It is acknowledged by Investor that the information provided by [Company] _____ is confidential; therefore, Investor agrees not to disclose it and not to disclose that any discussions or contracts with the [Company] _____ have occurred or are intended, other than as provided for in the following paragraph.

It is acknowledged by Investor that information to be furnished is in all respects confidential in nature, other than information which is in the public domain through other means and that any disclosure or use of same by Investor, except as provided in this agreement, may cause serious harm or damage to [Company] _____, and its owners and officers. Therefore, Investor agrees that Investor will not use the information furnished for any purpose other than as stated above, and agrees that Investor will not either directly or indirectly by agent, employee, or representative, disclose this information, either in whole or in part, to any third party; provided, however that (a) information furnished may be disclosed only to those directors, officers and employees of Investor and to Investor's advisors of their representatives who need such information for the purpose of evaluating any possible transaction (it being understood that those directors, officers, employees, advisors and representatives shall be informed by Investor of the confidential nature of such information and shall be directed by Investor to treat such information confidentially), and (b) any disclosure of information may be made to which [Company] _____ consents in writing. At the close of negotiations, Investor will return to [Company] _____ all records, reports, documents, and memoranda furnished and will not make or retain any copy thereof.

_____   _____
Signature   Date

Name [typed or printed] _____

[Investor's Company] _____

This is a business plan. It does not imply an offering of securities.

*There's a certain Buddhistic calm that comes from having
...money in the bank.*

— Tom Robbins

Funding Your Plan

While navigating your new or existing business on its intended road to success, there are many varied funding paths you can take. This section will help you conduct informed evaluations of capital in the right places, and early on, before your funding needs jeopardize your business. The insights presented here can give you leverage and advantage over someone else who may begin the process only when already desperate for immediate financial assistance.

Funding Your Plan includes:

- Identifying Your Capital Needs
- Narrowing the Search for Funds
- Self Funding
- Locating Private Resources
- Tapping into Commercial Funding
- Parting Tips

■ Identifying Your Capital Needs

Identifying your capital needs and seeking the right source of financing for filling those needs can get confusing and complicated at times. You may have started in business as a specialist in a particular area of business-marketing, sales, R & D or operations. Now as an owner or manager you need at least a general understanding of all aspects of business, especially appropriating and making efficient uses of funds.

The basis for your business may be a very sound concept, but funding new growth or maintaining existing growth can pose many challenges. Different types of capital requirements need different funding vehicles, all with different rules and steps similar in many ways to a game of monopoly or chess. Growing a business most often requires more capital than is readily available from existing cash flow or from the resources of the founder(s). Conversely, obtaining too much capital or raising it too soon can also cause other problems for the business.

The first step in this search is to learn and understand the pros and cons of the various types of capital needed by your enterprise. Capital comes into your business in two ways: as Equity capital or as Debt capital.

Equity financing is the investment of the owner(s) in the company. It stays in the company for the life of the business (unless replaced by other equity) and is repaid only when and if there is a surplus in the liquidation of the business—after all creditors are paid. Usually getting new equity is very difficult, especially during the early stages of the business.

Debt financing, on the other hand, can come into the business in a variety of ways. It comes for a defined period of time and is paid back with some form of interest.

The financing of your business can be further classified as start-up financing, which is usually equity, working capital financing and growth financing. Start-up financing is the financing to get the company to an operational level, including the costs of getting the first product(s) to market. This is best done with equity and long term loans or leases.

Working capital is required to drive the day-to-day operations of the business. In most businesses the operational needs vary during the year (seasonality, inventory buildup, etc.) and the working capital tides over the fluctuating expenses involved with doing the base business.

Growth capital is not tied to the yearly aspects of fueling the business. Rather, it is needed when the business is expanding or being changed in some significant and costly way that is expected to result in higher and increased cash flow. It is generally longer term than working capital and is paid back over a period of years from the profits of the business.

Knowing specifically what type of capital your business will be needing will put you in a stronger position when evaluating how and where to seek your financing.

■ Narrowing the Search for Funds

Next you need to become familiar with the pros and cons of the various sources of financing and how each might cater to your specific capital needs. Are you an established business needing to buy fixed assets such as a new building or new equipment? Or do you need to add a new line of inventory to your stock? Are your needs for short-term money to help you through a seasonal cash crunch? If so, the typical source of financing for these kinds of needs is a traditional commercial bank.

If you are starting a new business and have sufficient collateral but need additional capital funds, the SBA loan program might be for you.

> **Note:** For loans under $100,000, the SBA has recently begun to ease documentation and collateral requirements to encourage and support small businesses. The SBA also is encouraging women and minority-owned businesses with its new quota system. (See SBA Funding Programs, page 128.)

However, if your proposed business is on the leading edge of technology, and there is a potential for substantial growth, venture capital might be the appropriate financing source. These types of funding are discussed later in this chapter. Knowing the specific needs of your business will help to significantly narrow the scope of your funding search.

The methods for keeping abreast of funding options available to your business include networking with industry colleagues and successful business leaders in your region, soliciting the advice of financial experts and reading financial publications. Many entrepreneurs and investors are now also turning to on-line financing services, which are appearing with greater regularity. Some of these services attempt to match small businesses with investors, while others electronically post lists of companies seeking investors and then allow investors to examine the lists for companies of interest. Usually both the businesses and the investors pay fees to have access to this service.

> **Note:** These activities will help keep you positioned for the right funding move at the right time. Keep a sharp eye out for creative ways in which other successful businesses, similar to yours, are handling their funding. Follow up any leads for funding ideas that hold promise for your type of business. Most of all, don't get stuck in a rut of focusing on only one type of financing. Keep your options open. Hold several cards that can be played at the appropriate time for your business.

The following is a description of many of the options available for funding businesses in today's economy. The most commonly used funding sources are described for you more fully than the less-used, narrower in scope methods. For your convenience, the sources have been generally grouped into the following categories: Self Funding, Private Resources and Commercial Funding.

■ Self Funding

The vast majority of businesses (close to 90%) are begun with less than $100,000 and close to a third are begun with less than $10,000. This kind of money is usually available to the motivated entrepreneur by taking a close look at the personal resources at his or her disposal well in advance. Several of the most common self funding methods are described here.

Personal Savings and Equity

This capital reflects the degree of motivation, commitment and belief of the founder in the enterprise. This type of investment also takes the shape of sweat equity, where individuals either donate their time or provide it at below market value to help the business get established.

Moonlighting

Many home-based businesses are begun while the founder is still working a regular job. The income from the job can both help support the owner during negative or low cash flow of the business set-up phase and it can provide working capital to augment the business' cash flow.

Home Equity Loans

This may be the fastest growing method of raising money for individuals. Banks generally are willing to lend up to 70% or more of a home's appraised value, minus any existing mortgage(s). For tax purposes, you can deduct interest on up to $100,000 of debt on home equity loans, regardless of how you use the money.

Insurance Policies

Some entrepreneurs have been known to completely cash in their life insurance policies. Many insurance companies have, in recent years, liberalized their criteria for allowing policy holders to borrow against the value of their policy.

Tax Deferred Retirement Accounts

Dipping into your tax-deferred retirement account can be a last resort for funding your business. This works best if you are more than 59 1/2 years of age. While the money in your Individual Retirement Account or 401(k) plan is technically available to you, you'll need to pay a 10% early withdrawal penalty plus regular income tax on money you withdraw. It might be possible to get an unsecured loan on the strength of your retirement accounts. Although these accounts would not directly be pledged as collateral, the money could be withdrawn at a later date to repay the loan if it was required.

Credit Cards

"Pulling out the plastic" for fast funding of your business is more viable now than ever before. MasterCard or Visa card holders with good credit now often receive credit limits of $10,000 and above. Credit card interest rates on cash advances vary considerably, from as high as 21% to 15% or lower. Annual fees can also range from over $50 down to zero. This means it is wise to investigate getting the best deal you can when obtaining your credit cards. It may be advantageous to close out one or more of your high interest cards and transfer the balances to lower cost credit cards. The Bankcard Holders of America (Suite 120, 560 Herndon Parkway, Herndon, VA 22070-9958) is a resource for information on low rate credit cards and building good credit.

Bootstrapping

Often the best money to go after is the money that can be saved from the current costs and overhead of your ongoing business. The process of thoroughly searching through your operation for opportunities of savings and improved efficiencies will also allow you to learn more about the intricacies of your company, which will put you in a position to manage it better—a double return on your invested time and effort.

Customers

Certain types of businesses can require an advance deposit from customers, which quickly spurs cash flow. If you can encourage cash payments instead of giving customers credit, you avoid financing them. Similarly, you can also facilitate receiving cash quickly by granting cash discounts for early payments by customers. In any case, the more quickly your success has an impact on your suppliers and customers, the more likely they are to offer such deals.

Stock Purchases and Options to Employees

Your employees can be your partners in solving needs for capital at your company in a variety of ways. You can offer certain senior and trusted employees to become common stockholders by investing in a purchase of your company stock. Employees usually have limited discretionary funds for stock purchases, but every dollar counts, and employee dollars usually come with the motivation to help improve the results of the company, thus the value of their investment. Common shareholders also have the right to have a say in the management of the company. Another possibility is to offer these employees nonvoting preferred shares of stock in return for their investment.

Employee Stock Ownership Plans

Companies can formally set up ESOPs (as they are called) to not only raise capital, but also raise employee morale and productivity. In a typical ESOP the employee is allowed, as determined by management, to purchase up to a certain amount of stock during a certain period of time. There are generally regulations about cashing in (redeeming) the stock if the employee should leave the company. An example might see an employee being able to have five percent or more of his or her weekly salary deducted for stock purchase after one year of employment.

■ Locating Private Resources

Just as it has in the past, reality suggests that the world of private investors, including friends, relatives, coworkers, wealthy acquaintances (angels) and various sophisticated individual investors, is a likely place to go to raise capital for your business. The total pool of all types of private investments in business is vast. For example, in 1992 in the U.S. the venture capital industry invested approximately $2 billion, while a variety of private investors invested perhaps 20 times that—$40,000,000,000.* As huge as this pool of money is, the forms that individual private business investments take are diverse as is the creativity of the people making the deals.

Choosing this private path leads to questions of how to find and inform a sufficient pool of potential investors about your need for private funding. Then, in exchange for the investors' money, what mechanism should be used to issue to them the documentation or securities that represent some equity or debt interest in your business? The key is knowing what aspects of deals are critical to your business and having multiple options available as you search for and enter into your funding negotiations.

Investment from Friends and Family

Next to personal savings, the second most popular source for start-up capital is friends and family. Often, they may not be as worried about quick returns as other outside investors would be. There have been many success stories from investments of friends and family. There is also a high incidence of problems associated with this source.

Because the process of due diligence is often not carried out with family and friends, problems sometimes ensue. Thus, receiving capital from such a consenting, informed investor is often better than from a rich, unsophisticated relative or friend. Your relative or friend may not investigate your deal carefully and, should problems occur with the business and investment, your relationship with them may suffer.

---

* Source: *Finding Private Venture Capital for Your Firm: A Complete Guide*, Robert J. Gatson, John Wiley & Son.

A wise policy is to provide the same disclosure to a friend or relative that you would provide to most sophisticated investors. Resist the temptation to keep things loose and undocumented. Draw up the terms, conditions and payment schedule in writing for their signature and yours. Even if you receive a "friendship loan" at no or low interest, provide documentation in return. This is the smart, professional business approach that minimizes the potential down side of unstated assumptions and their implications. As a result of formalizing your deal, your relationship with your friends and family will have a much better chance of remaining intact.

Angels

If you are a small business and you only need limited amounts of capital, seeking the type of private investor called an "angel" might be the best alternative. Over 700,000 angels invest over $30 billion of equity in small businesses each year. These people generally invest in the $25,000 to $50,000 range, but sometimes you can get more by dealing with several "angels" at once, since they sometimes prefer to invest as a group.

Angels have sometimes been called the "invisible" segment of the venture capital industry. Networking through trade associations, civic organizations and your business community may lead you on the path to an interested angel. With individuals you have a tremendous amount of leeway in structuring the investment. You can structure it as debt or equity and vary the terms and repayment. Sources of personal investors go beyond family and friends.

Previous or Present Employer

Your employer may not want to lose your abilities and contributions, should you decide to start your own business. There are situations where this employer can become your first major customer. This can be solidified with a purchase order if you are going to be providing manufactured goods, and also a specifically worded work-for-hire agreement if you are to provide services to your past employer.

In another situation, your employer may agree with you that it would be wise to spin off an idea of yours into a new company. Providing funds in this type of venture of yours may be a sound investment for the employer, who should already know the market, the competition and your abilities and motivation.

Individual Partners

This is a way to join forces with one or more individuals to expand the capabilities of the business. Like a marriage, the partners bring different, and hopefully complementary, resources to the business. For example, one may bring technical expertise, while the other may bring the primary financial resources. Another desirable match may be to team a person who has administrative abilities with a person who has strategic vision.

A partnership can be a way to get a business up and running while one or both partners still have other work or business commitments. It may also be effective in the early stages of business growth or in turnaround situations.

Corporate Partners

A growing trend in the '90s sees small businesses forming partnerships with larger corporations. Most Fortune 500 companies are now involved with these arrangements as a part of their corporate strategy. In this model, the larger corporation becomes a minority owner of the smaller company.

As a small business you receive the advantage of access to capital. You may also receive, as you grow, access to some of the resources of the larger company, such as distribution capabilities and product development opportunities that could act as formidable barriers to entry for potential competitors of yours. Your partner company gets into attractive markets and will share in your profits.

Strategic Alliances

In an effort to quickly put together a profitable project, it is becoming more commonplace to have two or more enterprises join forces for collaborative work. A popular book, *The Virtual Corporation,* by William H. Davidow and Michael S. Malone, touches upon this concept in detail. With businesses becoming more complex and global every day, and with increased emphasis on specialized knowledge and on fast new product development, partnerships are increasingly emerging among companies and entrepreneurs. The movie industry has modeled the concept of strategic alliances for decades. Diverse talent is sought and brought together for a common, defined project. After the movie is completed, many contributing elements to the production are quickly disbanded.

Private Foundations

With determination and the ability to prove that a "charitable" investment in your enterprise will have positive social impact, benefiting more than just you, finding funding from a private, nonprofit foundation is possible. While some foundations fund entrepreneurs directly, most foundations give money and support services to nonprofit organizations, which seek to accomplish the foundation's mission by coordinating and supervising the distribution of these resources in exchange for the specialized work needed.

Private Placements

In the United States, there are only two ways to legally offer (sell) the securities of your company to investors: 1) the transaction must either be registered with the Securities and Exchange Commission, as is done when a company "goes public" in the traditional sense, or 2) it must be exempt from SEC registration, often referred to as a private placement or limited stock offering. Due to the considerable legal requirements and the large commitment of time and money involved with a registered Wall Street public offering, many companies may not be ready to go public, and others may not ever want or need to do it. In recent times exempt offerings are becoming more viable alternatives for companies in search of early funding.

If your company is a viable candidate for offering securities to private investors via private placement, you must have prepared the proper documents you need to comply with federal and state securities laws and regulations. Upon completion of paperwork and proper filing, you'll need to identify potential investors, market your offering to them and, most importantly, track your results. By going through this process you will (1) be equipped to generally evaluate your fund-raising situation, (2) determine where you may need help, (3) become knowledgeable of current exempt offering issues and regulations, (4) perform the necessary preparatory steps and (5) generate proper documents to effect a Private Placement for your company.

Limited Partnerships

If you know who your investor(s) will be ahead of time, a limited partnership may be an easy, relatively fast and inexpensive way for you to create a business partnership. This form of raising money for business usually involves one general partner who represents the business owner or management team and several limited partners who remain generally silent and inactive in the operation of the partnership.

Emphasis in limited partnerships by investors has shifted away from tax write-offs toward yield and safety, with a renewed interest in them as a hard-asset component of balanced portfolios.

■ Tapping into Commercial Funding

One of the greatest benefits of our free enterprise system of supply and demand is the vast network of diverse, targeted funding vehicles that has evolved. It has been fine tuned over recent decades to provide specific types of capital to different businesses in different industries and regions. The opportunities to turn business dreams into reality are in large part carried out through various channels of this vast, commercially based funding system.

Commercial Banks

In addition to lending money in various ways, banks also provide their business customers with various accounting, collection, payroll and bookkeeping-related services (for fees). These outside services are often less costly than doing it yourself...another way of minimizing your need for additional financing.

The Guarantee of Repayment

Because of the conservative nature of lending, a loan officer usually looks for two primary repayment sources plus collateral. The only way a bank can be repaid is with cash. The first source of repayment is the historical ability of a business to produce more cash than it uses. Profits plus depreciation do not equal the cash a business produces each year. Other factors like the collection of accounts receivable, the expansion of inventory, and the payment of accounts payable must also be considered. Bankers will also look at the personal credit history of the owner in many business situations.

The second source of repayment is the apparent ability of the business to produce enough cash in the future. A banker knows that past performance is no guarantee of future potential (ask Eastern Airlines, Chrysler, or International Harvester). The banker will look to see how solidly the cash flow projections have been put together, how knowledgeable you are about the cash coming into your business and how it's being spent, and your ability to avoid a cash shortage.

Even if a business meets these two requirements, a good banker will still look for a third source: personal guarantees or collateral, anything you can show that is available as security for repayment of the debt. Examples of collateral are stocks and bonds, equipment, savings account passbooks, accounts receivable, or the cash value of life insurance policies. Remember, banks are not real estate brokers. They don't want to have to sell your property, they want cash.

Given the conservative nature of banking, those companies with established track records (this excludes new businesses) looking to finance expansion or seasonal changes in cash are the perfect candidates for bank loans. They have the proven ability of past performance, they are able to reasonably project the future and they usually have collateral. The sound business usually has the three repayment sources required by a bank.

Successfully Applying for a Loan

With a general understanding of how banks and bankers operate, how do you successfully apply for a loan? The best way is to prepare a complete loan package.

The first page of the loan package should list how much money you want to borrow, how long you want to borrow the money for, the rate of interest you expect to pay, how the money will be used (purpose) and a brief statement of why you need the money (cause). For example, you need to borrow $25,000 for inventory. That is the use or purpose of the loan. The cause is the addition of a new product line and the resulting sales growth.

The package should include a page or two history and description of the business. It should state when and where the business was opened, who the owners are, and how the business evolved to where it is today. It should discuss who your customers are and how you market to them. This section also includes a description of your products and services and a statement about your competition. The description of your competition should list their strengths and weaknesses and what sets you apart from them.

Next, you need to discuss your future goals and objectives for the company. This section will include in more detail how the borrowed money will be used and the effect on the company. Inclusive in this section is a set of budgets that will illustrate the future ability of your company to repay the note.

Lastly, you need to include copies of at least the last three years' financial statements and IRS tax returns for the business, your personal tax returns for the same period and your personal financial statement. If you are offering any type of collateral, a description of that should also be included.

SBA Funding Programs

Contrary to popular belief, the U.S. Small Business Administration is alive and well. For those small businesses looking for start-up funds, the SBA might be the best approach. The SBA provides its broad-based Loan Guaranty Program as well as a variety of special financial programs.

SBA Loan Guaranty Program

The best approach for SBA financing is to find a commercial or savings bank that is a certified SBA lender. Although any bank can apply for an SBA guarantee, most do not have the appropriate staff or training to process the applications or monitor the loans according to SBA guidelines. However, those banks that are certified SBA lenders can usually get a response from the SBA in a matter of days.

Under this program, the SBA does not directly fund the loan. What the SBA does is to guarantee up to 80% (sometimes up to 90%) of the loan for the lending institution, to a maximum of $750,000. Although there is no specific break in the interest rate charged, one advantage for the borrower is the ability to repay the note over an extended period of time. The SBA generally caps rates at 2.25 to 2.75 points over prime, plus a fee equal to approximately 2% of the loan. Close to a quarter of SBA loans go to start-up companies.

In order to qualify for the SBA guarantee, the borrower must first be considered credit worthy under normal lending guidelines. The SBA is not in the business of guaranteeing bad loans! Once the lending institution accepts the credit, it recommends it to the SBA. As traditional bank financing to small businesses has become increasingly difficult to obtain, the popularity of SBA loan programs has grown tremendously. In 1993, close to $6.5 billion of SBA loans were made, more than double the 1988 level.

Typically, the SBA prefers to finance new businesses or the acquisition of existing businesses. It does not like to refinance existing debt and in order to do so, the borrower must be able to demonstrate a significant hardship caused by the existing debt relationship. The SBA does consider guaranteeing mortgage loans for buildings occupied by the business owner.

The SBA offers many services, like the Small Business Development Centers and the Service Corps of Retired Executives (SCORE), to help entrepreneurs put together loan packages. Check these services out before turning to the professional "loan packagers." If you need professional assistance, ask your bank to recommend a loan packager. They charge around $1000 to $1500 to complete the volumes of paperwork. Look at the track record and ethical practices of anyone you consider.

A final remark about the SBA concerns the Small Business Development Centers. These organizations are partially funded by the SBA and by state governments. Although not in the business of lending money for small business, this organization is an excellent source of information. They offer all kinds of continuing education courses and one-night seminars specifically for the business community. These courses are usually free or require only a minimal fee. The SBDC also offers free counseling. They will not write your business plan or find the best location for your business, but their core of experienced counselors are usually superb sources of advice and guidance. The SBDC is organized on local levels and has offices at about four dozen universities and junior colleges. To locate an SBDC look in the phone book under the U.S. Government listings for the office nearest you.

Microlenders

In the '90s microloans have become popular in areas where ready access to business funding has traditionally been limited. Microlender programs tend to be revolving funds offering a few hundred dollars to $25,000 loans. This money is usually provided at high market-rate interest and is often coupled with training and technical assistance to the qualifying entrepreneur. Thus, this vehicle for funding should be used cautiously as a resource if traditional loan sources do not prove to be helpful.

The SBA has its Microloan Program, which began in 1993, that bypasses banks and works through a network of community development (primarily nonprofit) corporations. Call the national SBA Answer Desk in Washington, D.C., (800) 827-5722 to obtain more information.

Venture Capital

The venture capital industry in 1994 was on a pace to match 1993's record total. After slumping to $1.7 and $1.4 billion in 1990 and 1991, respectively, the $3.1 billion raised by venture capital in the U.S. in 1993 equaled the previous high established in 1987.

Venture capitalists are usually looking for high growth candidates in certain niches in which they specialize their expertise. A large portion of venture capital investments are poured into technology and health care companies. VCs (as they are called) assume relatively high risks. One-third of their investments are partial or total losses, a third are between break-even and two times cash on return, while the other third of VC investments realize returns of greater than two times. The big winners have to make up for all the losers and marginal performers.

Even if you do fit their narrow parameters, their money often comes with various demands, including specific performance requirements, legalities to comply with, and often intrusion into your company's goals and operations. Typically, they want to see proprietary and protected technology (patented), opportunity for significant growth, a clear "exit strategy" (go public, be an acquisition, leveraged buyout or merged within 5-10 years, etc.) and most importantly a cohesive, seasoned and committed management team. They bet as much on the jockeys as they do on the horse. That includes sometimes replacing jockeys—which could be you. They will want a comprehensive business plan, but it better grab their attention in the first couple of pages or else they'll toss it. These guys play hardball, so you'd better be prepared to play their way. This is often a very narrow option not available to 99% of businesses.

Some of the most common ways to raise venture capital funding are described in the following paragraphs.

Venture Capital Funds. Venture capital usually refers to a fund or pool of money established for the sole purpose of making an equity investment in small, high growth companies. The VC fund accepts and manages investments from individuals and invests that money in small companies with high growth prospects.

Investment Banking Firms. Venture capital is also raised occasionally by investment banking firms. Traditionally, investment bankers concentrate on investment in established, larger companies; however, they do invest in specific new ventures in emerging growth industries. They'll typically form a syndicate of investors for a qualifying venture proposal. Deals with investment banking firms generally start in the $5 to $10 million dollar range on up.

Boutiques. A variation on investment banking firms are investment "boutiques." The "boutiques" operate on a smaller scale, aiming at local or regional companies who need capital in the $1 to $10 million range. They raise funding for ventures through private individuals, banks, finance companies and investing their own capital.

Venture capitalists like businesses on the leading edge of technology or new industries. They like to see the potential for sales to at least double on an annual basis and the possibility of a multimillion-dollar industry being developed. The advantage of venture capital over bank loans (asset based lending) is that they don't have to be repaid. It is an equity investment.

The repayment does lead to a major concern of venture capitalists. Their investment is not permanent. They usually like to fund the company for five to ten years and then want to be bought out. They are not long term investors. Therefore, part of the initial offer must be the objective of going public or being purchased by a larger company. Either way, you must be able to prove that the fund will be able to find a ready market for their investment at some point in the intermediate future.

The venture capitalist is taking a large risk that your company will fail altogether or will not grow sufficiently so that they can sell their stock. For this risk, they require a substantial return on their investment. This return can be in the form of dividends during the growth phase or might be in the form of a substantial profit on the sale of the stock. Either way, expect the venture capitalist to want a big chunk of the business and a big return on his investment.

Going Public

For certain companies with proprietary products or unique services in "hot" industries, an Initial Public Offering (IPO) or selling shares to the public is an enticing yet expensive way to obtain large amounts of capital. This market was booming in the mid-eighties, then went into the doldrums after the major stock market setback in 1987, and is now somewhat returning to prominence in the mid-nineties.

On the positive side, going public is a way to obtain cash for significantly growing a business quickly. It is also a way for the CEO/owners to "cash out," to pay off debt and the stock option reward to key employees, and to attract top notch talent into your company. Achieving success after an IPO will help facilitate additional fund acquisition for equity increase or more favorable terms on future borrowing. Mergers and acquisitions may also be more easily accomplished with stock transactions instead of using cash.

Proceeding with an IPO is a major decision that requires much specialized expertise, 18 to 24 months to execute and significant expense. An investment banking company typically underwrites the deal and may collect from six to ten percent of the offering's gross proceeds. Legal and accounting fees often top $100,000 for an IPO, as can other printing and registration fees. Other down sides to an IPO are high levels of required disclosure of information to the government and to investors, some loss of owner's control and management flexibility, higher susceptibility to a takeover and short term pressure on performance/dividend.

Franchising

In the U.S., there are over a half million franchised outlets that account for over a third of all retail sales. Internationally there may be over 100,000 more. It has been a very fast growing phenomenon, especially during the last couple of decades. Franchising involves a franchisor, who owns, produces or distributes a particular product or service, who grants exclusive local distribution rights to a franchisee, who agrees to certain standards of business and who provides a payment or royalties to the franchisor.

As a funding method it can be looked at from two directions: as a franchisor you can extend your existing business to multiple locations and areas; as a franchisee you can quickly start a new business or speed up the growth of your existing business. From both directions franchising involves using another person's or business' capital to mutually expand one's own business. In addition to funding benefits, both parties can grow because of standardized marketing, name, controls and facilities. Each can benefit from the inherent economies of scale. As a franchisee you can view this situation as one that lessens the overall risk of getting into business.

The International Franchising Association provides in-depth information on franchising. There are a variety of books, periodicals and trade publications that list franchising opportunities and the issues surrounding them. Your local newspaper classifieds may be a good place to start looking for what may be available in your area.

Commercial Finance Companies

Commercial finance (or loan) companies have evolved out of large manufacturing companies that established subsidiary companies to finance the parent company's receivables. Many of these financing subsidiaries grew successfully to the point that they began using their surplus funds to provide similar services to other companies.

For companies who get turned down by commercial banks, commercial finance companies will often be more accommodating. Because these finance companies are willing to make loans to relatively high risk borrowers, their loan rates are generally higher than commercial banks and other sources. Credit lines usually run at prime rate plus 2% to 6%, plus a closing fee in the range of 1%.

A revolving credit line is the most popular form of funding offered by commercial finance companies. They are almost exclusively secured lenders requiring collateral, and usually advance up to 80% of accounts receivable or inventories. Some commercial finance companies are also involved with fixed asset financing and factoring. (See the Factoring and Leasing sections that follow.)

Factoring Companies

Factoring is a method of receiving money as a loan based on your accounts receivables. The factoring company, in effect, buys your company's accounts receivable and then either provides money on the date invoices come due or advances money before the invoices come due.

Large factoring firms generally charge a commission of 1-2% of the total dollar volume of the invoices bought. If advancing funds, which usually is up to 80% of the value of the invoices, the factoring firm charges 2-3% above the prime rate. While factoring is relatively expensive, it is a way to generate needed cash in a hurry. The factoring companies are proficient at knowing the credit track record of your customers, since they interface directly with them in collecting on their loans to you.

Leasing

During the last twenty years leasing has become a popular form of receiving funding by using your acquired assets as security. Leases work best when the leased asset involved is usable for a long term, has value independent of use at your business and takes relatively little management time or effort if the item should be reacquired at the end of the lease or if you default on payments.

Leases can be arranged through many asset suppliers or through third party companies that deal primarily with the financial aspects of the deal. In an operating lease situation, the leasing company owns the equipment and provides services such as repair and insurance. In a financial lease, you are responsible for the services while the lessor merely owns the equipment.

Veterans Administration Guaranteed Loans

As a benefit to honorably discharged veterans, the Veteran's Administration has long offered a small business loan guaranty program similar to the SBA Loan Guaranty Program. The Veteran's Administration will work with you to guarantee the majority of your loan in order to help your chances of loan approval through traditional lending avenues. Look in your phone book to locate the Veteran's Administration office closest to you.

■ Parting Tips

Recurring themes throughout Part 4 have been about learning the financial needs within your company and also becoming aware of the various alternatives of financing that are available to you. Look at these issues early and often as you develop your business. Read, ask, look and listen. If having sufficient capital to grow your business stays high on your business priority list, the opportunities will be there for your benefit.

Be inquisitive and open minded, yet be cautious and safe. Check on both the institutions and people with whom you may be dealing. Know their track records during both the good times and bad times of their other customers. Know about second sources for any financing path you may intend to follow.

■ Review Questions

1. What is start-up financing? What are the three main capital components of start-up financing? Would you expect to get them all from the same source of funding?

2. What is the main source of funding for the vast majority (close to 90%) of businesses that are begun with less than $100,000? Why is this such a popular method?

3. What are some common private resources? Why are private resources so important?

4. What is a private placement of stock?

5. What is the SBA Loan Guaranty Program?

6. What type of companies are venture capital firms seeking? What level of risk are they generally willing to accept?

■ Activities

1. Throughout this entire text you have been using your potential business or current business as an illustration in the end of section activities. Now that you have done all of the underlying work for your business plan, what type of capital do you need – equity, debt, working or growth? How much of each? Considering all of the options covered in this chapter, which funding sources will you pursue and why?

2. Triad Distribution is a small warehouse operation in central Illinois with plans to establish a huge regional distribution center for gourmet and specialty food items. Triad would sell directly to grocery and discount supercenters, delivering the product with its own fleet of trucks. The one giant distribution center would be highly computerized and use robotics to select and pack orders. The center would be able to supply a ten to twelve state area.

   Triad is working on a business plan. Initially $1 million will be needed to finance the continued study of the concept, draw up plans, and pursue customers and financing. Next Triad will need $40 million to fund the building and pay for software development. Most of the equipment and trucks will be leased, but another $2 million will be needed for deposits and down payments. In addition, working capital for inventory and payroll will need another $7 million.

   As an outside consultant to Triad, write a memo suggesting appropriate sources for these capital needs. Be specific as to which sources would be best for various needs and why.

Do not let time pass without accomplishing something.
Otherwise you will regret it when your hair turns gray.

— Yue Fei

Appendix A: Using BizPlan*Express*

Appendix A will help you install BizPlan*Express* quickly and easily. It covers these topics:

- What You Need to Use BizPlan*Express*
- What's On the BizPlan*Express* Disk
- File Compatibility
- Installing BizPlan*Express*
- Word Processing and BizPlan*Express*
- Spreadsheet Processing and BizPlan*Express*

For technical support using the BizPlan*Express* files, call South-Western College Publishing at 1-800-543-0174.

■ What You Need to Use BizPlan*Express*

You need the following equipment and software to install and use BizPlan*Express*:

- An IBM-compatible 286 PC or higher with:
  - 4 MB RAM
  - 2 MB free hard disk space
  - 3.5" high-density floppy disk drive
  - Windows 3.1 or Windows 95
- Word processing software (see page 137)
- Spreadsheet software (see page 137)

■ What's On the BizPlan*Express* Disk

Your BizPlan*Express* disk contains word processing and spreadsheet template files to help you write your business plan.

Word Processing Templates

BizPlan*Express* contains the following text templates:

Top 20 Questions	0-20QUES
Title Page	1-TITLE
Table of Contents	2-TOC
Executive Summary	3-EXECSM
Vision and Mission	4-VISION
Company Overview	5-COMPNY
Product Strategy	6-PRODCT
Market Analysis	7-MKTANL
Marketing Plan	8-MKTPLN
Financial Plan	9-FINPLN
Cover Letter	COVERLTR
Non-Disclosure Agreement	NONDISCL

Depending on which format you select during installation, the files have the extension .DOC or .RTF. See File Compatibility on page 137.

Spreadsheet Templates

BizPlan*Express* contains the following spreadsheet templates:

Gross Profit Analysis	PROFIT
Budget	BUDGET
Income Statement (Yr 1 by Month)	INCOME1
Cash Flows (Yr 1 by Month)	CASHFLW1
Balance Sheet (Yr 1 by Month)	BALANCE1
Income Statement (Yrs 1-5)	INCOME5
Cash Flows (Yrs 1-5)	CASHFLW5
Balance Sheet (Yrs 1-5)	BALANCE5
Break-Even Analysis	BREAKEVN

Depending on which format you select during installation, the files have the extension .XLS or .WK1.

■ File Compatibility

Word Processing Files

The BizPlan*Express* word processing files are supplied in three different formats:

- Microsoft Word 2.0 for Windows (.DOC)
- WordPerfect 5.1 for DOS (.DOC)
- RTF (Rich Text Format) – used for transferring formatted text documents between applications and between platforms (.RTF)

Since the installation program asks you which of these formats you want to install, you need to determine the format that works best with your word processor. The following table lists several of the most popular PC word processors, and shows our recommendation for the BizPlan*Express* file format (from the formats in which BizPlan*Express* files are supplied) that will work best with those word processors. This is the file format that you should specify during the installation process.

If your word processor is:	Select this option:	To install text file templates in this format:
Ami Pro 3.0 for Windows	1	Word 2.0 for Windows
Claris Works 1.0 and later (Windows)	1	Word 2.0 for Windows
FrameMaker 3.0 and Later	1	Word 2.0 for Windows
Microsoft Word 2.0 and later (Windows)	1	Word 2.0 for Windows
Microsoft Works 2.0 and later (Windows)	1	Word 2.0 for Windows
Professional Write	2	WordPerfect 5.1 for DOS
Q&A 4.0	2	WordPerfect 5.1 for DOS
WordPerfect 5.1, 6.0 for DOS	2	WordPerfect 5.1 for DOS
WordPerfect for Windows	2	WordPerfect 5.1 for DOS
Ami Pro 2.0 for Windows	3	RTF
Microsoft Word 3.x and later (DOS)	3	RTF
Microsoft Works 3.0 for DOS	3	RTF
WordStar 6.0, 7.0	3	RTF

Spreadsheet Files

The installation program provides two spreadsheet installation options:

- Option 1 installs the financial statement templates in Microsoft Excel (.XLS) format.
- Option 2 installs the financial statement templates in Lotus 1-2-3 (.WK1) format.

◼ Installing BizPlan*Express*

Important: Since BizPlan*Express* is a set of files and not a software application, the Setup program cannot create a BizPlan*Express* Windows program group or icon. The BizPlan*Express* files are simply installed on your hard drive in a directory named BPEXPRS (or whatever directory name you specified during the setup procedure) and may now be accessed through your word processor and spreadsheet programs.

If your hard drive is something other than C and/or your floppy disk drive is something other than A, use the correct letter in place of C and/or A in these instructions.

1. Insert the BizPlan*Express* Disk into the floppy disk drive.

Windows 95

2. Click on the Start button, then select Run.

3. From the Open Command line, type A:\SETUP and click OK. In a few moments, the Welcome to JIAN! window displays. Click OK when you are ready to continue. Go to step 4.

Windows 3.1

2. From the Windows Program Manager, select File, then select Run.

3. In the Run window Command line, type A:\SETUP and click OK. In a few moments, the Welcome to JIAN! window displays. Click OK when you are ready to continue.

4. Select the types of templates you want to install:
    *   text file templates
    *   financial spreadsheet templates
    If you select only the financial spreadsheet templates, go to step 6.

5. Select the option that lists the name and version of your word processor (See table on previous page). Click OK.

6. Select the financial template option that lists the name and version of your spreadsheet program, then click OK.

7. Install creates a default installation directory, C:\BPEXPRS. You may specify a different hard drive or directory if you prefer. Click OK. The install program installs the templates in the directory you specified.

Removing BizPlan*Express*

The BizPlanExpress Disk installs a program (UNSTALL.EXE) that allows you to remove BizPlanExpress from the hard drive or directory that you originally specified.

■ Word Processing and BizPlan*Express*

This section contains instructions for using the word processing templates with three of the most popular Windows-based word processors: Microsoft Word for Windows, Microsoft Works for Windows, and WordPerfect for Windows.

If you use a different program, check the on-line help or the manual for instructions about importing the .RTF files. If you need technical support, call South-Western College Publishing (1-800-543-0174).

Microsoft Word 2.0 and later (Windows)

The BizPlan*Express* text files are Microsoft Word for Windows 2.0 files. You can open, edit, save, and print them as you normally would any Word for Windows document.

Follow these steps to open any of the BizPlan*Express* .DOC files:

1. Start Microsoft Word for Windows.
2. Select File, then select Open.
3. In the Open window, double-click on C:\ in the Directories listing. Next, double-click on BPEXPRS. The BizPlan*Express* text filenames appear in the Files box.
4. Select the .DOC file you want to open (for example, 0-20QUES.DOC). Word opens the file and displays it on the screen.

Microsoft Works 2.0 and later (Windows)

Follow these steps to convert the BizPlan*Express* files from Word 2.0 for Windows to Works for Windows format. After you convert the files, you can open, edit, save, and print them as you normally would any Microsoft Works document.

1. Start Microsoft Works for Windows.
2. Select File, then select Open Existing File.

    3.0 Users: Click the Open Existing File icon on the opening window.
3. On the Open menu, double-click C:\ in the Directories box. Next, double-click on BPEXPRS.
4. Under List File of Type at the bottom left corner of the window, click on the down arrow key to scroll through the options and select Word 2.0 for Windows. The File Name scroll box now displays a list of BizPlan*Express* .DOC files.
5. Select the file you want to open (for example, 0-20QUES.DOC), then click OK. Works converts the file into its internal format and displays it on the screen.
6. Select File, then select Save As. Make sure the Save File As Type option is set to Works WP.
7. Change the filename extension from .DOC to .WPS, then press Enter.
8. Select File, then select Close.

To retrieve one of the newly converted BizPlan*Express* .WPS files, follow steps 2 and 3 above. Make sure the List Files of Type box displays Works WP (*.WPS), then select the BizPlan*Express* .WPS file you want to work with from the File Name scroll box.

WordPerfect 6.0 and 6.1 for Windows

Follow these steps to convert the BizPlan*Express* files from WordPerfect 5.1 for DOS to WordPerfect 6.0 or 6.1 for Windows format. After you convert the files, you can open, edit, save, and print them as you normally would any WordPerfect for Windows document.

1. Start WordPerfect for Windows.

2. Select File, then select Open.

3. In the Directories box on the Open File menu, double-click C:\. Next, double-click BPEXPRS. The Files box lists the BizPlan*Express* .DOC files.

   If the Directories box is not displayed, click the Quick List button in the Open File window. Select Show Both from the list that appears. The Directories box should now display.

4. Select the file you want to open (for example, 0-20QUES.DOC), then select OK.

   WordPerfect for Windows displays a Conversion in Progress message, then opens the file and displays it on screen.

5. Select File, then select Save. The Save Format window opens, asking you in which format it should save the file. WordPerfect is selected as the default.

6. Click OK to save the file in WordPerfect for Windows format.

7. Select File, then select Close.

To retrieve one of the newly converted files, follow steps 2 through 4 above.

■ Spreadsheet Processing and BizPlan*Express*

This section contains instructions for using the spreadsheet templates with two of the most popular Windows-based spreadsheet applications: Microsoft Excel (4.0 and 5.0) and Lotus 1-2-3 for Windows.

If you use a different program, check the on-line help or the manual for instructions about importing the files. If you need technical support, call South-Western College Publishing (1-800-543-0174).

Microsoft Excel 4.0 and 5.0 for Windows

When you select option 1 in the installation process, BizPlan*Express* installs the spreadsheet files in Microsoft Excel (.XLS) format. You can open, edit, save, and print them as you normally would any Excel file.

Follow these steps to open any of the BizPlan*Express* .XLS files:

1. Start Microsoft Excel.

2. Select File, then select Open.

3. In the Open window, double-click on C:\ in the Directories listing.

   4.0 Users: Select BPEXPRS from the Directories list and click OK.

   5.0 Users: Double-click on BPEXPRS.

   The BizPlan*Express* spreadsheet filenames are displayed.

4. Select the .XLS file you want to open (for example, PROFIT.XLS) and click OK. Excel opens the file and displays it on the screen.

When you are finished with a file, remember to save and exit the file before opening another file.

Lotus 1-2-3 Release 4 and 5 for Windows

When you select option 2 in the installation process, BizPlan*Express* installs the spreadsheet files in Lotus 1-2-3 for Windows format. You can open, edit, save, and print them as you normally would any Lotus 1-2-3 for Windows spreadsheet.

1. Start Lotus 1-2-3 for Windows.

2. Select File, then select Open.

3. On the Open menu, double-click C:\ in the Directories box. Double-click BPEXPRS and click OK.

4. Select the file you want to edit (for example, PROFIT.WK1), then click OK. Lotus 1-2-3 displays the file.

Nine-tenths of wisdom consists of being wise in time.

— *Theodore Roosevelt*

Appendix B: Resources

William Alarid, *Money Sources for Small Businesses.* Santa Maria, CA: Puma Publishing Company, 1991.

C. Gordon Bell with John E. McNamara, *High-Tech Ventures, The Guide for Entrepreneurial Success.* Reading, MA: Addison-Wesley, 1991.

Gustav Berle, *SBA Hotline Answer Book.* New York: John Wiley & Sons, Inc., 1992.

Kenneth Blanchard, Patricia Zigarmi, and Drea Zigarmi, *Leadership and the One-Minute Manager: Increasing Effectiveness through Situational Leadership.* New York: William Morrow, 1985.

Laurie Blum, *The Complete Guide to Getting a Grant.* New York: Poseidon Press, 1993.

Laurie Blum, *Free Money for Small Businesses and Entrepreneurs.* New York: John Wiley & Sons, Inc., 1992.

Stephen C. Brandt, *Entrepreneuring, The Ten Commandments for Building a Growth Company.* New York: NAL Penguin Inc., 1982.

William B. Bygrave, *The Portable MBA in Entrepreneurship.* New York: John Wiley & Sons, Inc., 1990.

Lawrence Chimerine, Robert F. Cushman, and Howard D. Ross, *Handbook for Raising Capital: Financing Alternatives for Emerging and Growing Businesses.* Homewood, IL: Dow Jones–Irwin, 1987.

William H. Davidow and Michael S. Malone, *The Virtual Corporation.* New York: HarperBusiness, 1992.

Drew Field, *Take Your Company Public! The Entrepreneur's Guide to Alternative Capital Sources.* New York: New York Institute of Finance, 1991.

Roger Fritz, *Nobody Gets Rich Working for Somebody Else, An Entrepreneur's Guide.* New York: Dodd, Mead & Company, Inc., 1987.

Charles L. Frost and Eugene E. Valdez, *How to Prepare a Bank Financing Proposal For Your Business (The Way a Banker Would).* Study Guide and Workbook. Valdez, Frost & Co, Business Finance Consultants, 1992.

Robert J. Gaston, *Finding Private Venture Capital for Your Firm: A Complete Guide.* New York: John Wiley & Sons, Inc., 1989.

Tom Hopkins, *How to Master the Art of Selling*. Scottsdale, AZ: Champion Press, 1982.

Lee Iacocca with Sonny Kleinfield, *Talking Straight*. Boston, MA: G.K Hall, 1989.

Seymour Jones, M. Bruce Cohen, and Victor V. Coppola, *The Coopers & Lybrand Guide to Growing Your Business*. New York: John Wiley & Sons, Inc., 1988.

Gregory F. Kishel and Patricia Gunter Kishel, *How to Start, Run, and Stay in Business*. New York: John Wiley & Sons, Inc., 1993.

James M. Kouzes and Barry Z. Posner, *The Leadership Challenge! How to Get Extraordinary Things Done in Organizations*. San Francisco: Jossey Bass, 1987.

Joseph C. Krallinger and Karsten G. Hellebust, *Strategic Planning Workbook*. New York: John Wiley & Sons, Inc., 1989, 1993.

Michael LeBoeuf, *The Greatest Management Principle in the World*. New York: Putnam, 1985.

Christopher R. Malburg, *All-In-One Business Planning Guide*. Holbrook, MA: Bob Adams, Inc., 1994.

Christopher R. Malburg, *Business Plans to Manage Day-to-Day Operations*. New York: John Wiley & Sons, Inc., 1993.

Joseph Mancuso, *How to Start, Finance and Manage Your Own Small Business*. Englewood Cliffs, NJ: Prentice-Hall, Inc., 1984.

Mark H. McCormack, *What They Don't Teach You at Harvard Business School*. Toronto, New York: Bantam: 1984.

Ronald E. Merrill and Henry D. Sedgwick, *The New Venture Handbook*. New York: AMACOM, 1993.

David Ogilvy, *Ogilvy on Advertising*. New York: Vintage Books, 1985.

Stephen M. Pollan and Mark Levine, *The Field Guide to Starting a Business*. New York: Simon & Schuster, 1990.

Al Ries and Jack Trout, *Marketing Warfare*. New York: McGraw Hill, 1986.

Al Ries and Jack Trout, *Positioning: The Battle for Your Mind*. New York: McGraw Hill, 1986.

Jerry M. Rosenberg, *The Investor's Dictionary*. New York: John Wiley & Sons, Inc., 1986.

W. Keith Schilit, *The Entrepreneur's Guide to Preparing a Winning Business Plan and Raising Capital*. Englewood Cliffs, NJ: Prentice-Hall, Inc., a division of Simon & Schuster, 1990.

Andrew J. Sherman, *One Step Ahead, the Legal Aspects of Business Growth*. New York: AMACOM, 1990.

Index